Gifts From the Porch Swing

EMBRACING GRACE AFTER LOSS

MARJI STEVENS

Mim's Pickety Press

Published by Mim's Pickety Press
a division of Embracing Grace Ministries
P.O. Box 5
Rush, NY 14543
www.marjistevens.com
www.EmbracingGraceMinistries.org

Edited by Rachel E. Dewey.
Initial front cover art by Hedberg Creative.
Final cover design and interior pagination design by Sandra Devaux.

Printed in the United States of America.

Ten-digit ISBN: 098868926X
Thirteen-digit ISBN: 978-0988689268

To Bill

And to those in need of the hope of healing after loss.

Life Chapters and Lessons

Find the Treasure

Dear Reader,

It's my privilege to welcome you to Marji's Porch Swing!

She's going to share treasures with you ... treasures of gifts God has given her.

I've known Marji for more than 35 years now, but I'll never forget the first time I ministered alongside her in Africa, observing the impact her music had upon the women I was privileged to reach there.

On that trip in 1984, I had taken Marji with me, in a box—a cassette tape of one of her recordings. On a hillside at a small "retreat center" in Zimbabwe, Marji's voice rose clear and true from my tiny tape player to the missionary women seated on rocks and grass during a personal devotional hour. Her music echoed across that hill, entering their hearts, and encouraging them in a time of weariness within and warfare around them.

In Uganda, I took "Marji in a Box" to the first women's conference held after 12 years of Idi Amin's cruel reign and slaughter of many of his people. As I played her singing, her music was like an ointment poured over the wounded women who had endured so much suffering.

I played Marji's music everywhere I went in Africa, promising to bring her back in person.

The next year, Marji herself traveled with me to Africa…and she ministered richly, leaving precious gifts in Uganda, in Kenya, and in Zaire (now the Democratic Republic of Congo).

MARJI'S GIFTS

Marji's gifts are tied up with variegated ribbons of fun, humor, laughter … and tears. Those at our Creative Word Ministries (CWM) retreats have loved her storytelling, her singing, and her Scriptural exhortations. Marji holds a treasure-trove of creative giftings, artistic expressions, rich emotions, and spiritual insights bursting forth and needing to be shared with a dry and thirsty world.

But I knew little of this when we first met and exchanged tapes (mine were teaching tapes, hers were music tapes) following a conference at Elim Bible Institute in Lima, NY nearly 40 years ago. Back home in South Georgia, as I traveled in ministry, a treasure was unveiled as Marji's lilting voice and vibrant melodies filled my car, and her life-giving lyrics filled my heart.

Marji's music pulsed with real-life emotion, with spiritual vitality, truth, and the tangible hope of redemption that springs forth from the love of Jesus. Something was happening to me as I listened, and I knew she had a purpose in my life beyond blessing me with her music.

When we met the second time, a year later, Marji had not expected me to remember her at all, though the Lord had put me on a "treasure hunt" to find her. Our conversation then took us into heart-level sharing. I felt her passion for Jesus, her love of the Word, and heard her clear choice to see His name lifted higher than her own. She held intense determination to follow her Savior no matter the cost. Again, I saw the treasure.

I knew we shared a kinship in the Gospel, including a vision for ministry to women. I invited Marji to be part of our ministry team at Watson Homestead in New York's Southern Tier the next year, and later in Michigan and Georgia. To this day, 34 years later, she shares her treasures at every CWM retreat.

Over the years, through her fun sharing, we fell in love with her "Big Bill," her two boys, her dog, her foibles, her antique house, her porch swing, her "yodeling sparrow" song, her Mimmy stories as a grandmother, her down-to-earth illustrations, and her heavenly inspirations.

TREASURES OF DARKNESS

Then we had the opportunity to see deep inside her broken heart when fun had fled and music had been all but lost, when fibromyalgia had captured her voice and her hands, when she could neither sing nor play piano or guitar, and when sorrow had overrun her soul. Life was hard and "Big Bill" was gone, and pain and loneliness and grief had come, and Jesus had a lot of healing to do. We watched for glimmers of light to shine to and through our treasure.

We watched when the out-flowing Marji withdrew into a studio, when the streams of creativity went underground, were diverted, and then came forth again in fresh outpourings of paintings and sketches and crafts and varied artwork and children's storybooks and other writing. But I kept asking Jesus to give us back her song!

Now to my delight, we've heard the sounds of fresh waterfalls of song and singing and worship and ministry, and we've seen the overflow in ministry and especially in the outreach to widows and others who have suffered loss. We've witnessed the restoration of health and strength and fun and trust and stronger-than-ever faith.

Now you will hold in your hand and set before your eyes and take into your heart the treasures that her Lord has given Marji to give to you in this treasure-trove called a book. They are treasures mined and refined through life's crosses and losses. They are life-lessons learned through morning-by-morning discoveries of new mercies and daily experiences of grace at work. They will doubtless invite you to walk through her rebirth of song and of joy, through her loves and her laughter, as well as through her tears, and especially through her sweet times with the Lord on the porch swing.

And you will see that Marji, my treasured friend, is a kaleidoscope of varied broken pieces, vibrant colors, and unique designs that have fallen into focus with the many turnings of life. Through this book, her songs, her artwork, and other expressions of ministry, she can help to bring color and design to your life, too—and draw you into a closer communion with her Lord and your Lord.

Enjoy the reading ... and find the treasure.

Blessings abundant,

Rev. Sylvia R. Evans
Creative Word Ministries
Lima, NY

Broken Pieces

Have you ever read a passage of Scripture, then found yourself wondering how it might have unfolded in real life? This happened to me one day while reading in John 6—it's the sole Gospel account of the feeding of the 5,000 that mentions the young lad with the lunch.

As I read, the story sprang to life in my imagination, as if projected in a vivid Technicolor movie reel. I'm not claiming that what I saw is fact, but how the Holy Spirit inspired me through it changed my life.

It started with a scene in an ancient kitchen. A mother and young boy were talking.

The mother turned from preparing food and said to her son, "I know you are always having to share with your brothers and sisters. So, today, I have made you a wonderful feast—just for you." She handed her son a sack full of barley bread and fish. "Find a shady place to have a picnic and eat as much as you want."

"Thank you, Mother," said the lad as he scrambled outside. He was thrilled, and set out immediately to find the perfect place to have his feast. He had *big plans* for that lunch.

The young boy wandered into the village and saw an unusual number of men crowded in groups talking. He could tell, just from their body language, that something had them upset. The boy got as close as he could, without being noticed, and listened to what the men were saying.

"They cut his head completely off—" a man exclaimed, swiping his throat with his hand.

"Poor John," said another, as he traced the dirt with his sandal, "he didn't deserve that."

Yet another man stepped forward and roared with rage, "All to please that vile woman!"

"Where was the Master when this happened?" said a young man shadowed by a much older man with a heavy beard. "What is He going to do about this?"

Who got their head cut off? thought the lad. *Was it John the Baptist? I heard mom and dad talking about him. And who is this Master?* His curiosity got the best of him, and he momentarily forgot the plans he had for his lunch. Instead, he followed the people as they went looking for Jesus.

Far in the distance, he saw the Master and His disciples coming down from a mountainous ridge toward the massive crowd of people. *Closer—I have to get closer,* he thought, holding tightly to his sack.

The lad snuck as close to Jesus and His disciples as he dared, to see what was happening.

"Phillip," said Jesus, "where are we to buy bread, so that these people may eat?"

Philip looked at the multitudes and shook his head, "Even two hundred denarii couldn't buy enough food for so many."

The lad was alarmed when one of the disciples suddenly approached him.

2

"What have you got in that sack, son?"

"It's m-my lunch," he replied.

"My name is Andrew," he said, bending at his knees and reaching out his hand.

As if in slow motion, the man bypassed the timid hand the lad extended in greeting, and picked up the boy's lunch instead. "The Master has need of this."

The boy didn't dare speak out loud what he was thinking as he watched the disciple walk away with his feast. *Hey! That's mine! I had big plans for that lunch.*

Now he was really curious. *Was the Master hungry?* The boy snuck behind the group of men huddled around the Master.

"I found a lad who had five barley loaves and two fish," said Andrew, pointing to where the boy had been, "but how can these help to feed so many?"

Jesus didn't explain what He was going to do. "Have the people sit down," He said.

The boy almost protested, but quickly covered his mouth with his hands. *Sit down for what?* A few minutes later, the massive crowd of men, women, and children had settled in groups of about 50 each, all spread across a green, grassy area quite unusual for that part of the country. Then, Jesus lifted up the bread and gave thanks to God.

Wow—that's MY lunch He's holding!

Jesus began to break the boy's bread into pieces and hand it to the disciples to pass out. The lad watched in awe as the food kept coming and coming.

My mother is amazing! he said to himself. *How did she get all that food in one small sack?*

The lad had never seen a true miracle before, and he wasn't sure who Master Jesus was. He just stared in wonder as the people ate and ate until they were full. There was even food left over.

I can't imagine that the story of the lad ended there. It doesn't seem at all like the Jesus I know to allow a boy's lunch to be taken out of his hands without having a word with him. Perhaps the conversation went something like this:

"That was a fine lunch you had, son."

The boy nodded his head with his eyes transfixed on the face of Jesus.

"I know you had big plans for that lunch."

How did He know? Again, the boy nodded.

"If you will trust Me with the broken pieces of your plans, I can shape a miracle that will bless the multitudes," said Jesus, squeezing the boy's shoulder with a warmth uncommon for strangers.

There were 12 baskets left over. Isn't that just like God? When we give Him the little we have, He blesses it and produces something immeasurable, beyond what we could have imagined.

What did they do with all those baskets of bread? Some say there was one basket for each of the 12 disciples, but that would leave the boy with nothing. I couldn't imagine Jesus doing that either. What we give to the Lord is multiplied back to *us*, so we have more to share.

The Scripture says, "Give, and it shall be given unto you; good measure, pressed down, shaken together, and running over, shall men give into your lap. For with the same measure that you measure, it shall be measured to you again (Luke 6:38, NIV)."

I like to think Jesus sent the lad home with all the leftovers. I can picture the disciples, each balancing a basket full of bread on their shoulders, following the boy all the way home to bless his entire family.

Imagine the mother's surprise when she sees her pantry filled with food. I doubt the disciples would leave without a word of encouragement: "Your son has blessed the Master; now the Master wants to bless you."

As I meditated on the promise of transformation when we trust our broken plans and dreams to Jesus, I felt His presence. He gently whispered to me:

Trust Me, daughter. All the broken pieces in your life won't stay broken when you put them in My hands. They are never wasted. I can take each broken piece and shape it into something wonderful to bless the multitudes.

CHAPTER ONE

Boy Meets Girl

I met Bill in my junior year of high school. He was dating my best friend, Kay, who lived in the house behind my family's home in Rochester, NY. Bill was in his third year of college and used to write her the most amazing letters. Kay would call me whenever one came in the mail, and we'd curl up on her bed reading it over and over. It was unanimous—Bill was perfect! He even had nice handwriting.

I didn't meet Bill face-to-face until Kay's family had a moving-away sale. Bill drove up in a navy blue Volkswagen Beetle, which was just about the coolest car I'd ever seen. When he stepped out of the car, stretching his 6'3" slender frame in full view, I took one look at his light blue eyes, fringed with long, black lashes, and was speechless.

"You must be Marji," he said extending his hand.

I couldn't answer. I just nodded awkwardly, hoping he didn't notice my cheeks flush. He was so handsome, and because I'd read all his letters, I felt like I knew him.

After Kay moved away, Bill phoned me. At first, our conversation centered on how much we missed her, but gradually the topic changed. When he asked me out, I first refused out of loyalty to my friend. Bill persisted. It was my mother who finally encouraged me to go out with him. It only took one date and I was in love. I could see myself living with him the rest of my life.

We spent hours talking. It was our primary source of entertainment. It's what we wanted to do. My mom used to tell me our conversations were too serious. "Just be in love," she said. But I wanted to know everything about him, his views on all parts of life. He was the first man I'd ever met who was a good conversationalist, and he was an amazing listener.

Education was very important in Bill's family, and his interest in my schooling made my grades shoot up to high honors in my senior year. Previously, I'd only been an average student. He made me feel confident about everything. Even the creative things I was involved with took on new life. My father had given me a guitar when I turned 16 and I had been singing in a folk group, but when Bill came into my life, my creativity began to soar. He had that effect on me. He made me want to be better. He was interested in everything I thought and felt. He didn't try to fix me; he just honored me with his attention.

We dated for two years and were married in 1967.

Bill was in the military at the time, and was about to enter Officer's Candidate School. I left home for the first time when we moved to Virginia. Strangely, I never missed home once, because home to me was anywhere Bill was.

After Bill became a lieutenant, he was transferred to El Paso, Texas. We chose to live off base, so we found a little apartment on the edge of El Paso, near the border of Mexico, for $79 a month. Our landlady, Ann

Murphy, was a Bible-believing, on-fire-for-God Baptist. She used to talk about trusting God. I'd never heard the term "born-again," as she called it. I knew that Jesus died on the cross and was resurrected on the third day because we went to church on Easter, but I didn't know what that had to do with the rest of life.

The first year of marriage, Bill and I had practically nothing. I can remember a few times searching around the apartment for change to buy bread, but it was like a game. Never once did I feel poor, or worry about finances. I knew Bill would take care of me. Things always worked out.

On our first wedding anniversary, I waited for Bill to come home to see the announcement I'd taped on the front door. It read, "Welcome Home, Daddy!" I peeked out the window to see his reaction. He read the sign over and over before it finally sank in and his face lit up with surprise.

He burst through the door and then quickly stopped and stared at me. It was as if I'd become this fragile creature he was almost afraid to touch. Then he reached out and gently put his hand on my stomach.

"Oh, man ... " he whispered, then put his arms around me.

It was as if I was giving him the greatest gift imaginable.

During my pregnancy, he treated me like I was the only woman in the world to ever have a baby. I was like fine china needing careful handling. I loved every minute of it.

Our son Kyle weighed 8 pounds, 11 ounces when he was born, almost a month overdue. He was a butterball of cuteness with fuzzy blonde hair that always stuck straight up. Bill proudly called him "my boy." There was a lovely new expression on Bill's face, one I'd never seen before—the gaze of a loving father. He never looked more handsome than when he was with his son.

Bill was about to be discharged and we were planning to move home to Rochester when there was a rash of home invasions and rapes on the military base. It always started with obscene phone calls. I received one such call one afternoon as I was feeding Kyle. I put it out of my mind and didn't tell Bill at first, but when the second call came a few days later, I let him know. That's when he told me what had been happening on base.

A week later, Bill was on guard duty overnight when I got another disturbing call. "You'd better get ready—I'm on my way," I heard.

I raced next door to tell my landlady. She got her .357 Smith and Wesson revolver and we spent the night in my apartment having our own guard duty. The man never came. When Bill reported it to his superior officer, he was told to send me home to Rochester immediately. Bill had only three weeks left before discharge, but his commander said it wasn't safe for me anymore. I packed and Bill put the baby and me on a flight home. He planned to drive home in a month to meet us.

This launched us into a whole new adventure. It had been more than two years since I'd been home. The grandparents were beside themselves with excitement. And just as Bill had promised, we were moving into Grandma Stevens' old farmhouse.

CHAPTER TWO

The Farmhouse

The first time Bill and I drove out to see the farmhouse, we were dating. A dramatic canopy of trees arched over the quaintest country road I'd ever seen. From there, Bill's car eased out onto an open road where old barns garnished rolling hills, and golden wheat fields stretched out like giant patches in a homemade quilt. Bill pulled to the side of the road in front of a small white farmhouse with peeling paint and rustic gingerbread trim.

"This is it," I remember him saying as he rolled down his window. "My father grew up in this house. Grandma Stevens lived here until just before she died. I used to visit every weekend and walk the fields with my shotgun. I love it here."

The house had been vacant for years after Bill's grandmother died. It was in serious disrepair. Huge oak, pine, and horse chestnut trees surrounded the property which backed up to 80 acres of rich farmland. Peonies peeked out from the spirea bushes along the narrow gravel driveway. A huge sugar maple canopied the side yard. There was a grey hay barn 50 yards behind the house.

"Look at that great side porch," he said wistfully. "I wouldn't mind spending the rest of my life sitting there with you," he added as he reached over to squeeze my shoulder.

"Let's look inside," he said, opening the car door. The porch door was slightly warped and opened with a slight jiggle of the door knob.

Walking into the kitchen was like stepping back in time more than a hundred years. We were greeted with smells of mustiness, wood stove, dirt basement, and old wallpaper. The glass in the kitchen windows was aquamarine and each one looked like they'd been hand-blown.

"Uh ... indoor plumbing?" I asked reluctantly.

"Sure, it's right off the living room."

The bathroom door only opened part way before banging against the commode. The floor leaned so far left it felt like you were standing in the tilting room of a house of horrors. None of that seemed to matter to Bill, as we continued to other rooms.

"Everything about this old place holds fond memories for me. I can remember Grandma Stevens sitting right there in her rocker." He pointed to the corner of the sitting room next to the radiator.

I felt like I was stepping into the essence of Bill himself. "I love showing you this place," he whispered as he took me in his arms and pressed his lips against mine.

We'd visited the farmhouse several times while we dated. After getting engaged, Bill began to talk about the farmhouse as our future home.

Frankly, I never cared where we lived—I just wanted to be with him. As his fiancee, I looked forward to the end of our long-distance relationship. No more trying to squeeze our feelings into letters. I could wake up every morning, roll over, and find him there.

Four years later, just as Bill promised, I stood on the threshold of that kitchen, a new mother, just 23 years old, holding his son in my arms. The house had undergone some changes since we first visited. Bill's folks had rented it to a self-proclaimed handyman who did a few "renovations."

The horizontal, wide-plank wainscoting in the kitchen was painted a grotesque fleshy pink, and the wallpaper above it was dotted with orange teapots and gold roosters. Some strips of paper had actually been hung upside down. There were recycled cupboards leaning haphazardly against one wall with a partial slab of grey Formica resting on top. The bare light bulb in the center of the room above the dangling pull chain still lacked a shade. The kitchen floor was just as dreary. It slanted south and the flecked brown linoleum boasted large holes down to the underlayment.

The handyman-tenant had also done some "plumbing"—all of which had to be replaced. The pipes in the basement looked like he'd left them hanging in mid-air, as if he'd started drinking at the beginning of the project and, by the end, was too drunk to remember which direction the pipes were supposed to be going.

Bill's mom, Bernice, and his Aunt Vivian had scrubbed the entire house with Lysol and Clorox, disinfecting every inch. They swept up pans full of dead flies and wasps, and scraped years of grease off the 1950s electric stove. There were no outlets in the kitchen for a refrigerator, so the ancient GE monstrosity was put in the back room, called a summer kitchen.

The parlor had nine windows and doors with foot-wide molding stained dark mahogany, and speckled with age. One door opened to a long, narrow hallway leading to a small bedroom. Then there was the front door, bathroom door, kitchen door, French doors into the second living room, and the upstairs door.

We were told there were four bedrooms upstairs, but two of them measured only 7 x 7 feet, and the third bedroom had no windows. The ceilings were low and the walls were uneven and crumbling. There was no bathroom upstairs, and further, *no* closets!

I grew up in a wealthy suburb of Rochester, the only girl between two boys. My childhood home had walk-in closets and wall-to wall conveniences. I was moving into a drafty, 165-year-old farmhouse with hooks instead of closets, no outlets, no locks on the doors and the only bathroom, off the living room, had a warped door that wouldn't close. The house seemed overwhelming to me at first, but I knew it would feel like home as soon as Bill returned.

A momentary foreboding pierced through my oversized expectations when a man showed up at the door with a box full of kittens. He introduced himself as the former tenant (the one who hung the wallpaper).

"Here, you'll need these," he barked gruffly as he shoved the box in my hands. "Mice ... ya got lots of 'em."

"Oh, but really, no thank you," I countered politely, returning the box. "We're not cat people."

"Well, ya will be soon," he snorted as he turned and retreated to his truck. "You'll wish ya took 'em. Take my word for it."

I hadn't thought about mice, and the idea made me shudder, especially because I was still sleeping on the floor. After that, I slept with the covers over my head.

We had more than an occasional mouse. A rodent highway went through the center of the house. I'd never seen a mouse dropping in my whole life. Now I was cleaning up pans full. Mice were not the only problem. In the first two years, we caught a mother raccoon nesting in the crawl space, a snake in the bathroom, one barn rat, piles of crazy flies, wasps, bees, moles and chipmunks, not to mention the possum that blocked the front door one night and wouldn't let us pass. This rather spoiled suburban diva was in for the education of a lifetime.

I had three weeks before Bill came home. I was being rudely christened by the sounds and smells of farmhouse life, but I was determined to make it lovely for Bill's return. I'd never painted walls before, but I figured it couldn't be that difficult.

With grand intentions, I bought gallons of cheap, flat white paint, and a roller, and started in. I painted over lumps, bumps, crumbly plaster, and wallpaper. No one told me you had to prepare surfaces before you paint. I thought that just meant you took the pictures down.

There were places where I could hear something crumbling beneath layers of wallpaper, but I rolled right over the top of it. Some rooms had huge cracks in the walls and chipping paint, so I bought a huge tub of spackling and smeared it on the walls with my hands, then painted over top of that, too.

There was no insulation anywhere in the entire house, so absolutely everything leaked air. The doors were oddly shaped, like puzzle pieces, squeezed into sagging archways. The floors in the living rooms had been painted around the edges of long-gone area rugs, and they pitched and dipped in different directions.

I was grateful for the indoor plumbing, even though the bathroom looked like something out of *Alice in Wonderland*. The room was extremely long and narrow with a 10-foot ceiling. It was decorated with 12-inch squares of black and white linoleum glued to the walls.

The wide, pine-planked floor, painted pink, pitched east, and you could see straight through to the basement through cracks in the boards. The ancient enamel bathtub was sandwiched between the commode and the sink, all on the same wall. I later discovered if you sat in the bathtub with three inches of water, one cheek would be wet, and the other dry!

Two days before Bill returned, the moving van came with our meager belongings: one chocolate brown Naugahyde (cheap, fake leather) recliner from Woolworth's; one small couch upholstered in a fabric with gaudy, giant green leaves; a single end table from a little shop in Mexico near the military base; a queen mattress with no box spring, and Kyle's crib.

I moved things around until I was satisfied, and placed some field flowers in a quart jar on the table. While Kyle was napping, I got a cup of tea and went outside to sit on the porch for the first time. I never guessed the history—and blessings—that would unfold on that crumbling cement porch. (As I write this book, it's been 50-plus years in this old house.)

I felt a wonderful peacefulness in my heart looking out at the perennials Bill's grandmother had planted over the years. I wasn't sure there was a God, but just in case, I said a prayer that He would bless our home.

CHAPTER THREE

Gift of God

A year later, I became pregnant with our second son. I was thrilled about having another baby, but Kyle had been four weeks late and there were complications during delivery, so I was fearful.

There was another angst gnawing in my heart: my younger brother, George, had been born with cerebral palsy. My mother also had a sister with cerebral palsy. Though the doctor assured me that it was not hereditary, the concern was never far from my thoughts. So again, I decided to try prayer.

"God, if you are real, please protect my baby and let it come on the day it's due."

To my amazement, on the exact date forecasted, I went into labor. Part way through labor however, there was fetal distress and I was rushed into surgery. The umbilical cord was wrapped around the baby's neck four times, choking him as if hung by a noose. Miraculously, Dr. Barney was able to cut through the twisted cord and bring the baby out safely. If the hospital had been very busy that day, or if Dr. Barney hadn't been sitting in the very next room, our baby could have died or suffered brain damage like my brother George.

"That was a close call," said the doctor the next morning. "You're a very lucky mommy."

Was I lucky—or was it an answer to prayer? Could it be? Did God really answer me?

Bill was relieved when he found me awake and smiling. "I was so worried about you," he said, then bent over and gave me a kiss.

Reflecting on the close call, the name Jonathan came to mind. I wondered how Bill would respond to the idea.

"Honey, I've been thinking about the name Jonathan. How does that sound to you?"

"I like it," he said with a big smile.

I looked up the correct spelling and was floored by what I read, "Bill, Jonathan means 'gift of God,' or 'given by God!'"

My heart was fluttering with an unfamiliar, almost other-worldly kind of joy. It was the same feeling I had when the doctor said I was a lucky mommy. My mind swirled with a mixture of questions and hope. It was as if some power had suddenly turned up the light on a darkened, internal screen in my heart. But before I could comprehend what was happening, a phrase from my childhood shadowed the light: "It's just your imagination, dear."

That phrase had been a frequent one in my youth. Mom would scold me for being "melodramatic." Any strong or unexplained feelings were deemed "just my imagination." I did have an active one, and a creative temperament (whatever that means), but I wasn't lying. I really did experience life this way. A stronghold of self-doubt grew in me, though that was never Mom's intent. Long into my adult years I questioned my feelings. *Is God really speaking to me? Or is it just my imagination again?* It made discerning God's voice especially difficult.

With a brand new baby in the house, all thoughts of God were quickly replaced by our busy life. We were a happy tribe of four. Our boys were raised outdoors, with mud and sunshine. We didn't own a television set until Jonathan and Kyle were five and seven years old. We splurged to buy a bulky, 12-inch black and white TV that brought the sounds of *Captain Kangaroo* and *The Three Stooges* into our world.

From all appearances, my world was perfect. That's why I couldn't understand the deep melancholy growing in my heart. I tried to talk to my mother about it, but she didn't know how to answer me. If she didn't tell me it was my imagination, she usually reminded me, "You just need to be more grateful. After all, look at your brother."

This went beyond my imagination or needing to count my blessings. I didn't understand the intensity of my thoughts and feelings. I had a wonderful family, so why was I feeling depressed? I felt guilty that I wasn't happy. I thought maybe I should start to exercise, or volunteer somewhere. Maybe I'd be happy *if only* my house looked better, or *if only* I ate healthier. Maybe if I lost weight, I'd feel better about myself. Something in me felt broken. I tried to be the perfect sister, daughter, homemaker, mother, and wife. I worked constantly in the house to make things nicer, but then felt guilty I wasn't spending more time playing with the kids. If they were naughty and I lost my temper or yelled, I was wracked with guilt. *I'm ruining them. I'm a terrible mother.*

The accusations were continuous. Nothing was ever good enough— or maybe I should say *I* was never good enough. Bill was happy with me, he frequently told me I was "doing a good job." I thought the void in my heart was because I needed to work harder, try harder, be better.

If you've ever made applesauce, you know you can only stuff so many apples in the pot before it all boils over. Well, that's what was happening to me. The stress of trying to be perfect was slowly pushing my emotions to their limit. It didn't help that Bill was so even-tempered. He had amazing self-control. He never flew into a rage. He never got depressed. He was able to make a confident decision and live with the consequences, while I questioned everything.

Bill had purchased a dog for the boys. It was against my better judgement, but I was outnumbered. In came Hershey, a chocolate brown Labrador puppy. With all I was doing raising two boys, and trying to salvage a broken-down farm house full of critters, training a dog was more than I could handle. I was also skipping meals to lose weight, so I was becoming deeply exhausted.

Months passed and the pressure of everything was bringing me to the boiling-over point. One day, I had just finished scrubbing the kitchen linoleum, when the dog ran in from our grassless, rain-soaked yard and shook pounds of mud in all directions. Mud sprayed up the wall, and on the cabinets. As I watched the dog bolt into the living room for another big shake, something snapped inside me. I heard a loud whistling in my ears and the sound of someone screaming in the distance.

Bill came running when he heard me. I was trembling so hard I could barely speak, and I had no control over the torrent of tears gushing down my face. I collapsed into his arms. *What's happening to me? Am I having a nervous breakdown? It's probably just my imagination. I'm just being melodramatic. I should be more grateful. Why can't I be better? Why can't I be better?*

Bill led me to the couch then ran for a wet wash cloth. He gently washed my arms and face, then stood over me and softly blew my skin dry. For the next week, he stayed close. Bill was a teacher and school was out for the summer, so we had lots of time to be together. He made new boundaries regarding the dog, and promised to be more attentive. I had the most thoughtful husband in the world, but instead of feeling grateful, it just compounded my guilt.

CHAPTER FOUR

Finding Jesus

I slept for days and finally stopped crying, but I was secretly worried about myself. Bill always listened, but I began to fear I was wearing him out. So I put a smile on my face and tried harder.

My friend Ginny was a bubbly, joyful woman, and even though she had terrible arthritis, I never heard her complain. Never complaining was held as the ultimate virtue in my family. Finally, I opened up to her.

"How do you do it?" I asked, with tears catching in my throat. She thought for a moment and replied softly. "I get a lot of help from my church."

Church? I hadn't been to church since I was in elementary school. I was still questioning the existence of God and church was the farthest thing from my mind. I startled myself when I asked, "Can I come with you sometime?"

A broad smile spread across Ginny's face. "Sure!" she exclaimed. We made arrangements to meet the next Sunday at the Henrietta First Baptist Church. I arrived late, and was mortified to discover the only seats available were way down in the front row. I couldn't see Ginny anywhere.

Now what? I have to sit way down in front? I knew no one. The usher handed me a bulletin and I walked down the center aisle. I felt everyone staring at me. They didn't get many visitors in this church, I guess. Especially someone wearing red, patent leather high heels and a lot of makeup.

The Pastor was Demar Bezant. He was 82 years old, and a former Greek and Latin teacher. He stood in the pulpit like a 5-foot-2-inch arrow of conviction and preached straight from his rather tattered Bible. I tried to listen but I was somewhat distracted by the sense that I'd stepped into a Norman Rockwell painting. It was surreal. The women of the church, mostly senior citizens, were clad in polyester with matching shoes and purses. I tried to look around, but there was no way to do it discreetly while seated in the front row.

Pastor Bezant was on a roll, raising his voice and thumping the podium. Then suddenly, from the congregation, I heard an elderly woman's voice, "Well, I can see Demar forgot his watch today."

He cleared his throat, with a "Thank you, love," and closed his Bible. "While every head is bowed and every eye is closed, if you would like to accept Jesus as your Lord and Savior, raise your hand."

There was something about this place that caused hope to spring up in my heart. I couldn't see how anyone could be this happy unless they were on something, coming off something, or anticipating going on something. I had no clue what it meant to ask Jesus into my heart, but I wanted to be a part of this group. I wanted to catch their happiness. So, I raised my hand.

It was then that I realized you can't trust Christians, because nobody had their eyes closed, and nobody had their head bowed. They were all watching the lady in the front row—me!

I was a celebrity overnight. Suddenly, a crowd of people began pursuing me, wanting to know all about me. It seemed I was the new sensation. But inside, I felt the strange sense that I was being handed a new beginning.

"We heard you singing, and we'd love you to join the choir."

"Would you like to come to our women's group?"

I said yes to everything.

I had no idea what it really meant to be saved, or the significance of the cross. They said accepting Christ changes everything. Being born again would be the end of my old life and all would be new and wonderful. I definitely felt different, but I still wasn't sure why. I concentrated on the idea that now I'd finally be happy.

Bill was quietly making fishing lures at the kitchen table when I burst through the screen door.

"Honey, guess what?" I exclaimed, holding my arms out for a hug.

He looked up at me, shrugged a quick hug, then his eyes went down to my shoes. "Red? Where did you get those?"

"Never mind the shoes, they were on sale. I just asked Jesus to come and live in my heart today at Ginny's church!"

"How nice—don't you think you have enough shoes?" Bill mumbled as he continued working.

"Someone gave me this Bible, too."

"Are you moving out to join a cult?" he joked.

"Can't you listen to me? I'm serious. Oh, never mind," I sighed as I huffed out of the room.

I didn't want to joke about it. Something had shifted inside me.

I wanted him to be happy for me and accept Christ, too. I didn't understand God had to open his eyes. I knew this time that what I was feeling was NOT my imagination.

No one explained that the new life I'd received had to be worked into me, that sanctification and the renewing of my mind would take time. Without understanding this, I just added one more task to my list of 1,001 ways to attain perfection. Now I had to be the perfect Christian, too!

Bill had a strong *religious* background, but didn't quite understand my enthusiasm about knowing Jesus and reading the Bible. At first, he said I was being ostentatious because religion was a private matter, but that didn't stop me from talking about Jesus constantly. I couldn't help myself.

Gradually Bill softened as he watched my transformation. When a 10-day Leighton Ford revival crusade, affiliated with Billy Graham's evangelistic organization, came to Rochester in 1972, Bill wanted to go. When they had the invitation to accept Jesus as Lord and Savior, we went forward together and dedicated our lives to following Christ.

Every weekend, Bill's parents came out to the farm to visit the boys. Bill's dad played with the kids while Bernice and I sat at Grandma Steven's oak pedestal table in the kitchen and talked. It was nearly impossible for me to avoid the subject of my faith. I was definitely ruffling the feathers of a long line of devout Catholics. Bernice's brother had been in the priesthood. Bernice herself taught in a Catholic school. Bill attended Catholic schools from kindergarten through grad school.

"Marjorie, you are NOT going to change me," Bernice insisted. "You have your religion and I have mine."

When Bill told her he'd been born again, I could see the heartbreak in her eyes. This only added to the tension between us. I was never convinced she approved of me. I was not Catholic, nor was I a college graduate, I had a creative temperament and I was too emotional—a definite sign of weakness in her mind. Though generous, kind, and ferociously devoted to her only child, Bernice was stoic and never displayed emotion.

Over the years, she implied repeatedly that emotional people are just uneducated, creative types who tend to be unstable, and short people were bossy and controlling. I remember one day opening a surprise gift from a friend. It was a tiny, handmade guitar. This craftsman suffered with arthritis in his hands and I knew it wasn't easy for him to make. I was so touched by the unexpected encouragement, I burst into tears. Bernice watched me silently from across the table then said, "Creative people—up one minute and down the next."

Bernice, whom the boys fondly referred to as their "Bamma," was a wonderful grandmother. She showed endless patience and interest in everything they did, and extended the same grace to me. Though our relationship was a bit tense at times, we had a polite and respectful friendship. I loved her, but we were both strong women and very different. I was sure *she* was the difficult one, the one who needed to change. I wouldn't be surprised if she had the same opinion of me. But God had the perfect plan. It would not be for years down the road, but God knew what to do to melt my heart.

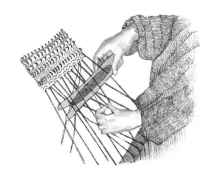

CHAPTER FIVE

The Weaving

It takes enormous faith to look into the face of death, or cancer, or divorce, and keep trusting that God has a plan. I can't explain why heartbreaking things happen, but I can tell you that God will never leave your side.

John the Baptist spent his life declaring Jesus Christ as the Lamb of God who takes away the sin of the world. John the Baptist walked in great self-denial, never treasuring the things of this world, and remained faithful and dedicated to God. He witnessed the Spirit descending upon Jesus, and boldly proclaimed He was the Messiah, the Son of God (John 1:29-30).

John the Baptist had the boldness of a lion. When he confronted Herod about his sin, John was wrenched from the open air of ministry, and thrown into a damp, dark dungeon, with little hope of release.

From his prison, John sent his disciples to inquire of Jesus, "Are you the Coming One, or do we look for another?" (Matthew 11:3, NKJV). Did John's trial make him question? Did he waver in his faith?

Jesus asked his disciples to carry a personal message to John in prison: "Go and tell John the things which you hear and see: The blind see and the lame walk; the lepers are cleansed and the deaf hear; the dead are raised up and the poor have the gospel preached to them. And blessed is he who is not offended because of Me," (Matthew 11:4-6 NKJV).

These almost seem like two separate thoughts. First, Jesus reminds John of all His miracles, but then says, "don't get offended?"

John was in a physical prison, but Jesus was reminding him to keep his spirit free. It was as if Jesus was saying "Don't let this trial entrap your spirit."

In my heart I heard: "My child, don't let the painful things in life that seem so unfair and so devastating steal your freedom in Me. Don't let trials put you in the prison of offense."

Paul Billheimer wrote an excellent book entitled *Don't Waste Your Sorrows*. He basically said we can learn from everything in life—even our deepest sorrows. The key is to stay close to Jesus. There are always rich principles of faith to be learned, and He will reveal them to us. From a posture of trust, we can learn from everything life brings our way. God will give us the tools we need to be victorious.

I remember one day as I was cleaning, a statement penetrated my thoughts. *Cuddle close, daughter. There are hard times ahead.* It startled me, and I couldn't understand. *Lord, is that You? What hard times?* A trickle of fear rose in my stomach and I stopped to pray. I made a notation in my journal. Several weeks passed before I had my answer.

My father had the type of job that required him to travel a great deal when I was growing up. At first, this was simply a part of life for me, and my brother, Bill, who was four years older. But things changed after our brother George was born with a diagnosis of cerebral palsy. The focus of the family became giving him the care he needed, and my father spent most of his time with George whenever he returned home from his business trips. George underwent multiple surgeries, painful physical therapy, and muscle spasms that put him in the hospital in traction. My parents were also struggling to find a school for him. Mother was exhausted and needed my Dad's help when he was home.

We were all thrilled when we learned Dad might be retiring. I thought I'd finally have a chance to get to know him better.

No one in the family knew he was having heart trouble—including my mother. Dad was a proud man and didn't like doctors. He believed he could solve anything with determination and positive thinking.

I was the first born-again believer in my entire family. I looked for every opportunity to share Jesus with them. My younger brother was the first one to accept Jesus. He was about 12 years old at the time. "Georgie, did you know there's a door in your heart? Jesus is knocking and wants to come in."

"I want Him in my heart," he said.

I was floored. "Oh my, don't be hasty," I replied, worried I hadn't read that far in the book I was reading on witnessing. "You think about it and I'll come back tomorrow."

The next day, we went into his bedroom and closed the door.

"Well, George," I said, "are you ready?"

George waved his hand in the air and responded in his usual, happy manner. "Oh, Marj, I couldn't wait for you. I couldn't fall asleep last night, so I asked Jesus to come into my heart and help me sleep—and He did!"

George was on fire for the Lord. He immediately began to work on my parents. He talked about Jesus all the time. He was excited to tell me one day "the Lord told me to drive my lawn tractor down the street because Mrs. Park needed my help. I helped her with all her groceries." You could tell how proud he was to have done what the Lord told him to do.

The admonishment to "cuddle close" wasn't far from my thoughts. Then, one morning in June, I awoke with a strange burden on my heart. I was struck with an overwhelming sadness. After Bill left for work and the school bus came, I got my tea and sat down to pray. The sadness grew stronger until I was weeping. Still, I had no understanding. It lasted until I had no more tears left.

The heaviness in my heart continued most of the day. Then Bill called. He was passing my parents' house on his way home from work and saw an ambulance in their driveway. He turned the car around and went to see what had happened. My Dad had been found in the yard lying under a tree. The doctors called it a silent heart attack. He was only 57.

"The neighbor is going to pick you up. I don't want you to drive," said Bill.

Lord, was this the reason for my sadness this morning? When I arrived, Mom and George were in shock. I knew that my weeping had been prophetic, tear-stained intercession, beyond my understanding, getting me ready for what was ahead. I had to be strong for them.

Before the funeral, the Lord said, "Don't wait until you are feeling weak to seek My help. Seek Me when you are feeling strong." So, throughout the day, when I felt as if I was handling things well, I'd separate myself. This kept me from being overwhelmed.

Back at my Mom's after the funeral, I went outside to be alone and sat near the tree where my Dad's body had been found. *God, why did Dad have to die now? I was finally going to get to know him? I don't know if Dad ever accepted You. How will I know if he is in Heaven?*

Suddenly I heard Bill's voice. "Marji, look behind you!" I turned around, and there was a brilliant, double rainbow stretching from one end of the sky to the other. "Will you look at that? It's a sign," Bill said. "Your father is with the Lord."

Bill's words were confirmed the next morning when a friend—who had no knowledge of the rainbow—called. "I was reading this morning, and saw this verse from Revelation 4:3 and I knew I had to call you. I believe it's for you," she said. "My version says, 'Those who stand before the throne of God will see a rainbow round about.' I could see your Dad looking at that rainbow and smiling at the Lord." Her encouragement was just what I needed.

Many loved ones die before we have confidence they knew the Lord. We can receive comfort from the Scripture that tells us, "The Lord is not slack concerning His promises ... but is longsuffering toward us, not willing that any should perish, but that all should come to repentance" (2 Peter 3:9, KJV). Our heavenly Father doesn't want anyone to step into eternal life without knowing Him. I believe He makes every effort to reach the heart of our loved ones, even as they lay on the edge of eternity, like the thief on the cross beside Jesus. "Then (the thief) said, 'Jesus remember me when You come into Your kingdom. And Jesus said to Him, 'Truly I tell you, today you will be with Me in Paradise'" (Luke 23:42-43, NIV).

One question lingered in my heart—why? I was thankful my Dad was with the Lord, but why did he have to die so young? We needed him. A couple days later, an unexpected newsletter came in the mail from the ministry of Corrie Ten Boom, a Dutch Christian who survived the Holocaust after losing her father and sister in the concentration camps. I'd read her book, *The Hiding Place*, which details how her family helped

Jews hide from the Nazis before they too, were exiled to the camps, but I wasn't even aware she had a newsletter—it just showed up. Included was Corrie's favorite poem, called **"The Weaver."**

"My life is but a weaving
Between my God and me;
I do not know the colors,
He worketh steadily.
Oft' times He weaveth sorrow;
And I in foolish pride
Forget He sees the upper
And I the underside.
Not 'til the loom is silent
And shuttles cease to fly
Will God unroll the canvas
And explain the reason why.
The dark threads are as needful
In the skillful weaver's hand
As the threads of gold and silver
In the pattern He has planned.
At last, when life is ended,
With Him I shall abide,
Then I can view the pattern
Upon the upper side;
Then I shall know the reason
Why pain with joy entwined,
Was woven in the fabric
Of the life that God designed

AUTHOR UNKNOWN*

*Editor's Note: While Corrie Ten Boom's book and newsletter did not originally state this poem's author, research in later years has attributed it to Grant Colfax Tullar, 1849-1950, a Methodist preacher from Massachusetts who later founded a publishing company which produced hymnals and Sunday school materials.

Tears caught in my throat as I realized it was God's perfect timing to have that newsletter arrive in the mail. *It's not my imagination. God truly is personally involved in my life.*

Losing Dad was like some of those dark threads, I thought. Music filled my mind as I read the poem over and over. I got my guitar and "The Weaving Song" became a jewel that I later recorded. It was definitely a gold thread in the weaving of my life—one of the miracles God shaped from the broken pieces of losing my Dad.

CHAPTER SIX

Excellence and the Ruddy Root

I was writing songs almost daily. Every time I picked up the Bible, melody floated across my mind. As more songs were born, more invitations were coming from churches of all denominations.

I thought if you were successful it must mean that you'd also be famous. Imagine my surprise when, instead of fame, God put a mop in my hands! He gave me a mop, an old farmhouse, two kids and all their friends, dirty dogs, and frustrating relatives. He wanted me to learn what it meant to be successful in His Kingdom. My ambitions needed to be pruned a bit and I needed to learn contentment. He wanted me to learn that serving my family was just as much ministry as going out to teach the Bible.

One day, as I stood at the kitchen sink paring carrots (a job I hated) my mind wandered again to the subject of success. *Lord, are You ever going to use me in a mighty way? I want to be powerful for You, Lord.* His answer surprised me.

When my kids were little we didn't have those neatly shaped baby carrots. We had to scrape, and cut from scratch. In 40 years of marriage, I figured out I pared two carrots four times a week for salads. Taking 8 carrots x 52 weeks = 416 carrots a year, x 40 years equals 16,640 carrots pared since I said, "I do."

Plus, I've packed 180 school lunches a year for two boys; that's 360 lunches for 13 years each. Those 4,680 lunches included two carrots per lunch, which adds another 9,360 carrots. Altogether, carrots for salads and lunches totaled 26,000 carrots, approximately 3,575 pounds. And I haven't even included picnics.

If it takes 30 seconds to pare and cut one large carrot, that works out to about 216 hours, or roughly nine complete days of my life paring carrots! If compared to the average 40-hour work week, it would take more than five weeks of 8-hour days to pare all 26,000 carrots. That amount of time investment deserves recognition—don't you think?

When I got my head out of the clouds, and my thoughts returned to paring the carrot, I'd scraped the thing right down to its middle.

"Oh Lord, I hate paring carrots," I sighed.

The Lord said, "I want *you* to be like a carrot,"

"A carrot? I don't understand."

"Like a carrot ... *Orange all the way through!*"

I examined the ruddy root, and sure enough, it was the same color and texture on the inside as it was on the outside.

Suddenly paring a carrot gleamed with pure significance. The back door slammed, and in dragged my weary husband.

"What a day!" Bill sighed, dropping his book bag and opening the refrigerator.

"Guess what?" I blurted out, way too chatty for my tired-out school teacher. "I was making a salad and the Lord told me He wants me to be like a carrot. What do you think that means?"

"Well, for starters, carrots don't talk!" he chuckled as he sauntered out of the room and upstairs for his usual after-work nap.

I was still chewing on my new inspiration when Sunday rolled around and it was my turn to share in children's church. I decided to tell the kids my carrot story.

"God can turn the most boring jobs into great adventures in learning." I expounded. "He wants us listening for His still small voice no matter what we're doing. You never know what He might say if you listen."

They watched me carefully as I pared a giant carrot. They seemed riveted to the idea that God spoke to me. As carrot slivers drifted onto the newspaper spread out on the floor, I explained how we can hear the voice of God.

"There are only a few times in history when God actually spoke to mankind in an audible voice. Most of the time, it's something you hear with your heart, and mind. We know God speaks to us through Scripture, but God also can put a clear thought in our minds. I can tell it's God speaking because it's always a lot smarter than me," I laughed. "He also speaks to us through our conscience. You know that funny feeling you get in your stomach when you're about to do something wrong? That's your conscience telling you to stop," I said putting a young man back in his seat. "Who can tell me why God wants us like a carrot?"

One little boy in the back of the room leapt up, enthusiastically waving his hand in the air. "I know," he announced, "it's because, God wants us to be delicious!"

All-the-way-through excellence is not about us striving to be perfect. Excellence is the result of abiding in Christ. God *wants* us to be branches

35

full of sweet Son-ripened fruit.

"I am the vine, ye are the branches: He that abideth in me, and I in him, the same bringeth forth much fruit: for without me ye can do nothing" (John 15:5, KJV).

Perfectionism is an unforgiving taskmaster. It's striving for something that doesn't exist, because no one can be perfect except God. Perfectionism is either black or white; it doesn't tolerate grey. It demands a perfect outcome. Excellence focuses on the process, not the outcome. Striving for excellence is a motivator and an encouraging force, while striving for perfection is disheartening.

God wants us to strive for excellence, but always from a position of acceptance—we are His children—even when we fall short. His goal is integrity of character and purpose, and integrity of motivation. It's learning to handle all the scrapes of life, from spills on a freshly mopped floor to times of deep discouragement and loss.

We can be our own worst enemy, expecting perfection from ourselves. Our journey in excellence begins the moment we embrace Christ as Lord. Our acceptance is a gift; it doesn't come through our performance (Ephesians 2:8-9).

Sometimes it was when I was feeling the farthest from victorious that I'd get an invitation to minister. I was always amazed. *How can You use me, Lord?*

I *never* felt qualified to do what I was called to do. I remember one time I'd just finished apologizing to my kids for losing my temper and the phone rang. It was an invitation to speak at a mother-daughter banquet. *Oh boy, I feel like the worst mother on the planet. Can't they find someone who doesn't explode so easily? I feel like a hypocrite, Lord.* But, the job description for ministry doesn't say only perfect people need apply.

Despite my inadequacies, one invitation led to another, first in neighboring towns, then out of town. The distance seemed to expand as my children got older.

CHAPTER SEVEN

Philip

The multiple roofs of Monroe Community Hospital, which also housed the county nursing home, etched a bleak silhouette against the dull December sky. The faded brick buildings boasted of expert craftsmanship once held in deep regard, but now they were just old and difficult to maintain. The wing for acute nursing care was home for hundreds of the elderly and the disabled. It was to be my next ministry assignment.

I first visited the county home with a group from my church. Christmas brought out the usual influx of carolers and visitors from all sorts of organizations. We sang and tried to create some holiday joy, gleefully exclaiming, "Jesus loves you!" Honestly, the entire scene depressed me.

During the holidays, it's good to include those who are less fortunate, but what about January and February, when the sun seldom shines around western New York, and nobody visits county home residents? A sudden chill of loneliness swept over me.

It was during this caroling visit that I met Philip. He was a small, fragile, hunch-backed man reduced to skin and bones. His head twisted permanently to one side, and he walked as if bent in pain. He carried a white towel over his shoulder. There was a presence about Philip that made me curious to know more about him. His handicaps were great, but his joy seemed greater.

As our songs of praise pierced through the depression of the stale, hot wing of that building, Philip began to weep. His joy and devotion was unmistakable as he lifted his hands to God in worship.

Several months later, I returned to visit Philip with my guitar. He seemed eager to welcome me. "How about a song, Philip? May I sing to you?" He lifted his hands into the air and began to cry and give thanks.

Through tears, we sang praise together for over an hour. Every once in awhile Philip would stop me. I couldn't understand all his words, but I grasped enough to know he was quoting entire, complicated sections of Scripture that he had memorized.

That day I dared to ask Philip how he came to live in this place. He explained that when he was 16, as he walked in the woods, he gave his heart to God. He stopped his story for a moment to cry and give thanks; then, blotting his tears with his white towel, he continued.

"I asked God what He wanted to do with my life." Without a pause, he added: "And he sent me *here!*"

Now Philip was more than 60 years old. He had lived almost his entire life in this place! "My life is His," he explained. "Whatever God wants for me is just fine."

A hush of reverence settled in my spirit as I said goodbye and drove home. I knew that I'd just experienced one of God's treasures. Philip understood the secret of contentment. There wasn't a hint of self-pity or regret. I only heard gratitude.

Although Philip remained a bright spot in my life, and I often spoke about him, the county home was such a sad place I really wasn't interested to return. Several years later, after singing at another facility in the community, my friend and I were driving home when she asked if I'd mind stopping for a minute so she could drop off something at the county home. I decided to just wait in the car while she ran inside.

Against the gray backdrop of the city, the trees around the massive building provided a touch of welcome shade for the residents. As I waited in my car, a clear and distinct thought seized my attention.

"Go sing to the man on the park bench."

My heart began to pound. I shifted in my seat, pushing out any notion that it might be God trying to direct me. The embarrassment of walking up to a total stranger and just starting to sing made me cringe. What would people think?

"What's more important to you, the opinion of man or being obedient to God?"

Caught off guard, I began to wonder. *What if God is telling me to do this?* Still trying to cushion my pride, I decided to wait for my friend to return so I could ask her what she thought. At least we could go together.

"Do you need an audience to do God's will?"

Still wrestling with doubts, I decided to take my guitar, casually walk over in that vicinity, and maybe strike up a conversation with him. Then, *if* the man seemed open enough—and I felt comfortable—I'd sing to him.

It was a bit of a walk, because he was sitting way at the back of the property. Drawing closer, I caught a glimpse of a white towel.

"Philip! Is that you?"

He immediately lifted his frail arms into the air and began to cry and praise God.

"Philip, is that you?" I repeated. "Do you remember me?

"I've been waiting for you," he said. "The Lord told me you were coming today!"

A little shiver ran up my spine. I sat beside him, and with the roar of the city behind us, I played my guitar and sang as Philip cried. It was a tender moment in a harsh world.

I don't know if Philip held a vision in his heart that was ever fulfilled, or if perhaps he dreamed of a different home. He never said; he just spoke of trust and thankfulness.

Philip has gone on to be with the Lord. He was an undiscovered treasure. Few knew he ever lived. The world would probably say that Philip was unsuccessful. He never appeared on television. No one ever invited him to speak to a group, or sit on a committee. He never owned a suit or a car, or had a career. He wasn't concerned about developing his self-esteem or realizing his purpose—all he had was a white towel to blot his tears, and a heart that knew God.

CHAPTER EIGHT

Two North

Meeting Philip had been such a blessing that I sensed the Lord encouraging me to visit again.

The county home was one wing of a large complex known as Monroe Community Hospital. That wing was reserved for long-term, chronic care patients.

On my first day, I went to see the chaplain to inquire about being a volunteer. The chaplain greeted me warmly and suggested that I choose one or two residents to be faithful to rather than trying to visit many and spread myself too thin. At his recommendation, I chose Nellie and Franny on Two North.

Juggling my guitar and a map of the hospital, I ventured out, excited to meet my new friends. As I made my way down the endless corridors toward Nellie's room on Two North, the sights and smells became overwhelming to me. I prayed for God's strength.

It was airless and oppressive. The halls were crowded with lines of parked wheelchairs, oxygen tanks, IV poles, linen carts and hampers.

Some residents sat amidst the clutter in their wheelchairs, trays in place, waiting for lunch to arrive. Padded restraining chairs barely held on to a few drooping patients. Sedated. Crying. Twisted. Frail. Withered hands reached out for me as I passed. Anxious voices called out, "Call somebody. Will you call somebody?" "Where's my daughter? Is she coming today?" "Get the nurse. I need my pills." "Oh, dear, they've taken my things. Will you find my things?" Sad eyes. Broken spirits. Overwhelming needs.

What am I doing in this place? How can I possibly contribute anything? The sadness was suffocating. My discouragement was growing by the minute. It was difficult to concentrate on finding Nellie's room. Skimming patient's names from door to door, I glanced into one particular room and saw an individual slumped over in a restraining chair. I paused for a moment, feeling strangely drawn to the sad figure silhouetted against the cloudy, hospital window. The name on the door read: MARIE.

Marie was very ill. A nurse was monitoring the elaborate machines that surrounded her. Marie's head was swollen beyond recognition. Her eyes were puffed shut, skin folds spilled over the neck of her gown. Except for a few stray wisps of gray hair, she was bald.

I can't handle this one. I thought, turning aside. *Besides, I've already been assigned to Nellie and Franny.* Pushing aside any consideration of Marie, I was relieved to find Nellie's room, just a few doors away.

Nellie was a large woman, with grey hair and long, carefully manicured nails. I don't know how old she was, but I'd been told she'd been bedridden for more than 30 years. She was blind and unable to walk, or even sit, without help. A Hoyer lift was needed to carry her from bed to chair, to bath, and back again. This was the extent of her daily routine. She was dependent upon the staff for accomplishing every physical need. Nellie was severely disabled, but she was just the kind of resident I wanted to visit. She wore flowery flannel housecoats and big plastic earrings. She was cheerful and pleasant to be with. Her room boasted of every visible sign of a loving family and friends. Cards and drawings from her grandchildren were taped all over the walls. Fresh flowers sat in a blue vase on her night stand and a wooden cross hung over her bed. Nellie was a Christian, and God's joy radiated from her.

We were instant friends. I started to play my guitar and sing, but Nellie stopped me. She was most interested in talking about her grandchildren. We shared for over an hour, then I went looking for Franny's room.

Franny was skin and bones. She was fortunate to have a corner room with a big window. There were no cards and pictures on Franny's wall. She had no flowers, no cross. Franny mostly complained. "They'll steal you blind here," she insisted. "I can't have anything in my room because they'll take it."

Franny was grateful that I'd come, and she quickly gave me a list of things for me to do. "I want a sweet roll from Bard's Bakery. Will you get me one?" That bakery was on the opposite side of town. I said I'd try.

"I've got to go, Franny. The school bus will be coming soon. I'll be back to visit."

"When?"

"Well, maybe next week."

"Don't forget my sweet rolls."

As I walked to the elevators I had to pass by Marie's room. I felt another tug in my heart. Again I resisted. *She's in a coma.* I rationalized. *She wouldn't even know I was there.* But driving home, I felt deep conviction that God was asking me to visit Marie. This time I agreed.

When I returned the next week, I was puzzled to find Marie's door closed so I went straight to Nellie's room. The privacy curtains around the bed beside Nellie were tightly drawn.

"Hi, Nellie! How are you today?"

"I've got a new roommate!" she exclaimed, recognizing my voice.

Just then, a nurse drew back the curtains and there lay Marie! A little shiver ran down my spine. Today *was* my day to visit her!

Marie was a sorrowful picture lying there. She lay motionless on a special waterbed to help protect her from bedsores. Fresh sheets were folded neatly across her wrinkled blue and white hospital gown. Lifeless. Unresponsive. Her face was still swollen, her skin taut and ashen. A feeding tube was taped securely to her nose. IV lines trailed along both arms.

Again, my heart was drawn with compassion. This time I couldn't run away. I studied her face. *There but for the grace of God am I.* I placed my hand gently on hers. "Hello Marie."

How could I have been afraid of her? She is God's child. She's in a coma but there's nothing wrong with her spirit. My heart was pounding. I picked up my guitar and began to sing. "Jesus loves you, this I know, for the Bible tells me so…"

One glistening tear formed at the corner of Marie's left eye and slowly trickled down her cheek. She moved her right hand as if she was trying to reach for me, but I knew that was impossible.

"Jesus loves you, Marie. He's right here. Don't be afraid." The tender presence of the Lord was so tangible in that room, it was hard to leave.

When I returned a week later, I was startled to find Marie's bed was empty. A nurse was helping Nellie into a high-backed wheelchair. "Good morning, Nellie, where's Marie?"

The nurse answered softly. "Marie took a turn for the worst, and last night she passed away."

"Oh no!" I gasped.

The nursed nodded and gave Nellie a tender pat on the shoulder. "We'll miss her, won't we Nellie?"

"Yes, we will," Nellie whispered.

Then the nurse turned to me and said, "Did you know that right after your last visit, Marie spoke for the first time in a whole year?"

"She said a word!" Nellie added.

"A word? What did she say?"

With an almost reverent tone of voice the nurse replied, "She said… 'Jesus!'"

"He's so faithful," Nellie whispered.

I was stunned.

The nurse left the room, and I sat beside Nellie. "I'm sorry you lost your friend, Nellie. You're absolutely right, God *is* faithful."

Two North provided a memorable classroom. God used Nellie, Franny, and Marie to teach me the importance of obedience, and His willingness to answer the cry of every human spirit—even in the last few hours of a coma. Marie never opened her eyes, but I believe with the eyes of her spirit Marie saw *Jesus* beside her bed, not me. With the faith in one glistening tear, Marie reached for His hand—and found Him there.

CHAPTER NINE

Africa

I was ministering in word and in song all over the northeast. It was clear to me that this was what God wanted me to focus on after meeting the needs of my family. In 1985, I was asked to accompany Rev. Sylvia Evans on a trip to Africa. She is a gifted teacher and exhorter with a worldwide ministry, and it was a wonderful privilege to travel with her.

Bill was supportive and excited that I had this opportunity. Bill taught African and Asian culture and history to high school freshmen, so there were some familiar parallels. The trip was planned for early summer. Bill would be out on vacation so he'd be home all day with the boys—now eight and ten. They had planned great adventures for the time when I would be away for three weeks. However, when I told Bill the dates Sylvia had planned, he said no!

"No? But didn't you say I could go?"

"Yes, but I don't feel peace about those dates. Tell her you can go if she changes the dates."

Oh boy, that seemed so presumptuous, but to my surprise Sylvia agreed to move the trip from July to June.

I questioned how Bill would manage that time because he would be right in the middle of exams, but he said yes.

Later, we learned Bill was being led by the Lord. If Sylvia and I been in Uganda in July, we would have been in the center of a violent coup as President Milton Obote was ousted from office.

The missionaries knew something was brewing at the time, but they kept the news from us. I remember hearing gunfire one night, but they told us it was due to a celebration somewhere. Fortunately, we were well on our way home when the violence erupted.

All our luggage arrived safely in Uganda—except mine. I overheard somebody say that it would be a miracle if I got my suitcase back at all, and if I did, it would probably come back vandalized. None of the missionaries wore my size, so I had no alternative but to wear the same dress day after day. It was dreadfully hot and we only had a quart of water for bathing every day. My dress was dry-clean only so I didn't dare try to wash it for fear it would shrink. Our hostess called the airport every day to check on my luggage.

Halfway through our week in Kampala, the capital of Uganda, a gentleman named David Polopolo, a Ugandan native, called to speak to me! He had just returned from studying music in the United States. While there, someone gave him a copy of my music, and he fell in love with it. How he discovered that we were in Uganda had to come from God.

"I have rented the Uganda National Theater for two hours to present my music to the nation. Kindly miss, would you come and sing? I will present my music in the first hour. You may have the entire second hour."

My thoughts immediately went to my dress. *But how can I stand on that stage in this sweaty dress? I have holes in my stockings, too.* As quickly as

I thought it, I knew the answer. There was no choice. To obey God, I would have to swallow my pride and just go.

I only had an hour to get there! There was no time to check the sound or warm up. I watched from backstage as the huge auditorium filled high into the balcony. David signaled for his choir to stand and the concert began. Their voices filled the room with glorious music for over an hour. After thunderous applause, David introduced me. I walked onto that enormous stage, trembling inside. I took comfort in the Lord's reassurance that language would be no barrier because His Holy Spirit would do the work. The lights nearly blinded me and I squinted to catch a glimpse of the audience. I signaled the sound person to start my accompaniment tape. With my first note, I could feel the anointing of the Lord come upon me, and my voice felt as if it was being oiled. The songs flowed out of me effortlessly.

My responsibility was no different in Africa than it was at home. All I had to do was lift my voice and worship Jesus as if He was the only One in the room. Later, I heard testimony that people had accepted Christ and some had even been healed while I sang. I simply worshipped Him in my dirty dress and torn stockings—He did the rest.

The purpose of our trip to Uganda was to lead a conference for women in leadership. Some of the women attending walked for days to get to the church. Many of them came with babies tied to their backs. They sat on hard, backless benches from morning until evening, hungry for the Word of God. I'd start the service with music and stories, then Sylvia taught from Scripture.

My suitcase was still lost, so day after day I wore the same dress. On the last day of the conference, my suitcase was returned in perfect condition. The missionaries assured me this was miraculous. I could hardly wait to change my clothes. When I opened the suitcase, I was overwhelmed with all the colors and choices. While grateful, I was convicted by the affluent abundance that lay before me. Most of the women at the conference had only one dress. As I lifted the first fresh garment from my suitcase, I had the distinct feeling that I was *not* to change my clothes. So, I pulled my dirty dress off the chair and put it on again.

That morning, when we entered the church, the women erupted with cheers. Two women approached me with big grins on their faces. They took hold of my arms, led me into another room, and started to undress me so I could change into a beautiful African dress they had sewn. I later learned they had been measuring me all week with the span of their hands each time we hugged.

The dress was a dark green, polyester print material with puffy sleeves and a high waist. It tied in the back and fit me perfectly. *Oh Lord, You are so good to tell me not to change*, I thought. Imagine the letdown if I'd come into the meeting that day wearing a brand new outfit. It would have ruined the surprise. When I emerged from the dressing room, the women erupted with cheers and whistles. God's joy was released, and when the music started, everyone jumped up to dance.

Through the interpreter, a woman told me, "You have taught us patience waiting for your suitcase." My old, blue dress had become a bridge that connected me with the women. It was as if that dress was an important uniform, an intercessory assignment. How could I have known losing my suitcase was a part of God's plan?

As we departed from Uganda, Sylvia was not feeling well. We continued on to lead another conference in Kinshasa, the capital of Zaire. It wasn't until we arrived that we learned our conference had been postponed to another date. Sylvia went straight to bed. I was missing home and wondered why God had brought me there if we weren't going to minister. That's when our hostess received a phone call from a Mennonite missionary nearby who desperately needed someone to visit her. I was available.

The woman wrapped her arms around me as she welcomed me into her home. "I can't tell you what this means to me. I've missed having a woman to talk to and I'm so lonesome for home."

We talked all day. She poured out all the frustrations that come with being on the mission field, and the tensions that had recently developed in her marriage. I realized this was another God-ordained assignment. It was amazing to realize that God would bring me from my little farmhouse in Rush, NY—and send me all the way across the world for one hurting woman. *Lord, Your love is so extravagant.*

Sylvia wasn't getting any better. We discussed staying in Zaire because Sylvia was not up for flying. However, when we went to the travel agency to postpone our flight, a stranger came up to us and whispered, "Don't cancel your flight. They'll tell you it's no problem to book another flight— but it's not true. You might not get out of Zaire for weeks and weeks."

We felt the Lord's definitive leading to go ahead and fly to Kenya, so we left the next day. Our flight from Zaire to Kenya was brutal. We sat for two hours on the runway in unbearable heat before the plane finally departed. Sylvia's fever was extreme and there was a worrisome look in her eyes. I had the sense things were far more serious than we knew.

We prayed our way into Kenya's main airport. We were the only women on the entire plane. Some of the men on the flight had guns. When the two of us arrived in Kenya, a precious missionary couple greeted us at the airport and strongly suggested Sylvia go straight to the hospital.

"We are so relieved you didn't stay in Kinshasa. You would *never* want

to be in a hospital in Zaire. Here things are much, much better." The
hospital physicians soon determined that Sylvia had typhoid fever
and amoebic dysentery.

I found a phone I could use and called home. Bill was very concerned
about my safety when I told him what was going on. "I want you to
come home now—it's time." My heart sank. I missed my family, but
going home was not the problem; it was leaving Sylvia. I felt I would be
abandoning her. Inside, however, I knew the Lord wanted me to agree
with my husband, so I promised I would try to get a flight home as
soon as possible.

It appeared that Sylvia was going to be in the hospital a very long time,
so I needed to make my own plans to get home—but how? I mustered up
the courage to call a taxi and travel, by myself, into Nairobi, the capital of
Kenya. I couldn't speak the language, but the driver understood enough
English to take me to the nearest travel agency. He waited as I walked into
the tiny, dingy office. "Excuse me," I said to a man sitting behind the only
desk in the room. "I need to book a flight to the United States as soon as
possible." He answered me in broken English.

"Sorry, Miss, we have no flights for you—no flights whatsoever." He
waved his hand, dismissing me.

Now what, Lord? Anxiety swirled in my stomach as the driver took
me back to the apartment. As soon as the door closed behind me, I
dissolved in tears.

"Lord, what do You want me to do?"

The next morning, God told me to go back to the *same* travel agency.

Once again, I called the taxi. The same travel agent greeted me in
the dingy office. "How may I help you, Miss?" He acted as if he'd never
seen me before. This time, his answer was completely different. "Sure, no

problem, we have flights for you—tomorrow is good, yes?"

Sylvia gave me her blessing, and the next day I began my trip home. I had no idea it would be more than a month before the doctors determined Sylvia would not get better if she stayed in Africa. A member of her ministry board flew all the way to Kenya to accompany her back home. Her recovery was slow but steady. God's faithfulness in every detail was amazing.

It took courage to travel the long way home from Africa by myself. I boarded the plane in my special African dress, handmade by the sweet Ugandan women. Two days later, the trip of a lifetime came to a close in the embrace of my husband and sons.

CHAPTER TEN

Sing Unto the Lord

Sometime after my journey to Africa, I was asked to sing for the International Christian Women In Leadership conference being held in Washington, D.C.

As the date approached, I grew more and more intimidated by the whole idea.

Washington? Lord, this is a big deal. Are You sure I can do this? It seemed every invitation was requiring more and more faith. He was putting me in places I would never have expected.

As I prayed about the Washington engagement, a picture came to my mind of a chubby bird resting on a branch outside a rundown house in the inner city. The little bird was not impressed or depressed about where it was. It simply lifted up its head and sang unto the Lord. Then the vision changed, and the little bird flew to a branch outside the White House. Again, the sparrow was not impressed or depressed about where it was. It just lifted up its head and sang unto the Lord.

My family was all excited about where I was going.

"Are you gonna see the president, Mom?" The boys were especially impressed. "Mom," Jonathan asked, "are you famous?"

That tickled me. "No," I said, giving him a big hug, "only to my family."

Butterflies swarmed in my stomach as I boarded the plane and flew to Washington, D.C. It wasn't until I arrived at the conference that I learned how formal the event was. *Oh no, Lord, another dress issue. I'm so underdressed,* I thought, tugging on my skirt to keep the hem even.

Women were streaming in with floor length gowns, fur shawls, and gleaming jewelry. I'd wanted to get a new dress, but our budget didn't allow it. The only new thing I wore was a pair of control-top pantyhose. At least I looked a little thinner. But trouble was on the horizon. I'd bought a small size, one too ambitious for my girth, and the mistake soon became apparent. During refreshments, I was balancing a cup and saucer in one hand and a plate of finger food in the other when I became aware that the top of my pantyhose was moving. The over-taxed waistband suddenly began to roll down! Now my polyester dress revealed the roll I'd been trying to conceal. As the elastic continued to descend over my stomach, I raced for the ladies' room to compose myself. Luckily, I'd saved the cookies on my plate, so I stuffed them in my mouth for a bit of comfort, then ducked into the stall to redress. That's when I heard the announcement for everyone to find their seats.

I blotted the tea that had dribbled down the front of me, checked my teeth for signs of cookies, and dashed back into the ballroom.

Crystal chandeliers spread shimmering lights all over the room. Three hundred women were seated at white, linen-covered tables. I scanned the room for signs of my hostess and spotted her waving from the head table.

Surely not the head table? Lord, hold my pantyhose up!

My place was next to Dee Jepsen, a Senator's wife who served as a White House liaison to women's organizations under President Reagan. Beyond her was Tammy Faye Bakker, the televangelist wife famous for her makeup and music. I was too nervous to eat, so I pushed my food around to make it look like I'd eaten something, and mentally ran through the words to my song.

As the program continued, the M.C. introduced that year's Dove Award winner followed by a long and impressive list of accomplishments. She approached the microphone with an air of confidence and fame. She wore a magnificent gown covered with sequins. Then she belted out her newly released song and brought the audience to their feet.

I slumped a little lower in my seat. *Lord, how can anyone follow that? I don't belong here.*

I hoped they'd forget me, but they didn't. I had no credentials and the biggest accomplishment I could think of at the time was giving birth to two nine-pound baby boys.

"Now, we'll hear from a little housewife from Rush, New York," the M.C. said. You could nearly hear crickets in the background as an unimpressed yawn rippled over the audience.

I gave my skirt a quick tug and walked to the microphone. I felt naked standing in front of that huge ballroom filled with some of the most famous women in Christendom. Before I could introduce my song, the sound man started my soundtrack. Then to my horror, as if someone signaled a breakout of chaos, the kitchen doors flew open and waiters streamed out to clear the dishes. People turned their backs to me and started talking. Even the women at the head table started talking. The Dove Award winner took one look at me, turned her back, and got everyone at her table talking. The noise in the room made it almost impossible for me to hear the music, but nobody was listening anyway.

Lord, did You bring me all the way down here to humiliate me in front of all these people? Couldn't You have done that in the privacy of my living room?

Suddenly, the image of the chubby bird flew across my thoughts, and I remembered. "Don't be impressed or depressed about where you are, just sing to the Lord."

Swallowing my pride, I lifted my head, and sang as if I were singing straight into Heaven. Slowly, heads began to turn. The chatter shushed as people stopped talking, waiters stopped working, and the anointing of God fell.

As my last notes settled over the audience, nobody moved. I walked to my seat in total silence. Tears of relief and gratitude trickled down my cheeks. The Lord turned their heads and arrested their attention—not my accomplishments, or what I was wearing.

This is who I am, Lord. I'm not supposed to be anything else but Your songbird.

Relieved to be back home with my husband and boys again, I told them all the details of my most difficult engagement. They listened wide-eyed as I told my story. Then, in typical Bill Stevens fashion, my husband said, "Now you know to wear socks next time."

My ministry invitations continued to grow. I was also being asked to conduct women's retreats. Every aspect of the ministry was growing. The idea of being famous no longer had an appeal. All I wanted was to follow the Lord and bring His presence no matter where (or in what dress) He sent me.

CHAPTER ELEVEN

On the Toes of My Father's Shoes

I'd just finished speaking at the New Hampshire State Women's Aglow retreat and my next invitation was in Pennsylvania. School was out for spring break so Bill was able to go with me. We had no idea just how important it would be that he was there.

We were booked into a lovely bed and breakfast, and after we set up at the church, we returned to our room for a quiet evening. Never once did we sense any warning that there was danger ahead. Neither of us were feeling the least bit unsettled.

I'd just written a new song. I knew from past experience that when the Lord inspired a new song before an event, it had an important purpose. Some of the lyrics were:

> When I'm weak, when I fall, I can count on You.
>
> You are always by my side to comfort and lift up.
>
> Lord, Your love is perfect. Mercy fills Your eyes ...

I made the assumption "fall" was pertaining to falling into sin.
I never took it as a literal fall.

The next morning before the event began, I placed my notes on the
podium, then turned to go down the stairs and return to my seat to wait
to be introduced. I had no idea that the bolts connecting the stairs to the
platform were unlocked. To my horror, as my foot landed on the top
step, the stairs suddenly moved. It was like teetering on a skateboard. The
steps collapsed. My feet went out from under me and I was catapulted
into the air. All I remember is the sharp blow to my back as I crashed
against the edge of the stage.

Next thing I knew, I was in a twisted heap on the floor, unable to
move. The pain was excruciating. Women rushed around me. I heard
someone calling the ambulance. Then, I heard Bill's voice, "You're going
to be all right, honey." Several women braced against my body to help
stabilize me until the ambulance came.

The ride to the hospital over bumpy roads and turns was a nightmare
of pain. All I could do was repeat the Lord's name over and over. It was
surreal. I couldn't believe what was happening.

The doctor immediately ordered X-rays. Muscle spasms sent
shock waves through my body as I was forced to hold still on
the hard X-ray table.

The nurse administered an IV with pain medication so I began to feel
a little relief. Bill was at my side.

"What would I have done if you weren't with me?" I cried.
He gripped my hand, soothing me with reassurance until I eventually
fell asleep.

I awakened to the sound of the doctor talking to Bill.

"She's severed a bone in her back at the waist. She is probably going to need back surgery to remove it."

Terror gripped me. I remembered when my brother needed back surgery, hearing my parents talk about how dangerous it was.

Bill called home and got the prayer chain started.

They kept me on painkillers and muscle relaxants throughout the next day. In the morning, the doctor told me I had to have another X-ray as preparation for surgery.

A few hours later, the doctor walked into my room with a huge smile on his face. "Well, Mrs. Stevens," he announced. "God has put the bone back on your spine! You will not need surgery."

The X-rays proved it. The bone was right where it belonged. "It's going to take a while for the spasms to quiet down," he said. "But I'm confident you will be able to go home in a few days, and in time, resume your activities."

We cried. Bill hugged me and whispered, "See, I said you'd be okay."

The next day, a woman from the church hosting the conference came to visit me with a startling report. "I *saw* the devil kick you, Marji," she said, clutching her Bible.

Later that same day, another woman from the church visited.

"Marji, I *saw* the devil kick you!"

I thanked her for coming and after she left, I asked the Lord what He thought. With total clarity, I heard Him say, "Don't worry. I have much bigger shoes. Just stay on the toes of your Father's shoes, and keep in the dance."

I understood immediately what He was saying, because one of my fondest memories as a little girl was dancing on the toes of my daddy's shoes. The only way to stay solidly balanced on his shoes was to keep my legs flexible, lean in, and never try to lead. If I tried to anticipate the next step, I'd slip off his toes. It was a clear picture of blind trust.

Every time a spasm would start, I pictured a conductor standing before an orchestra. He would tap his music stand to signal it was time to start, then raise his arms in the air and, with the downbeat, the music would begin. In my imagination, I could see Jesus walk up to me, extend His hand, and invite me to dance on His toes.

Focus on Me, daughter. Feel My arms holding you. Hear the music of Heaven surrounding you. I will dance you through this.

A friend drove all the way from Rochester to northern Pennsylvania with his camper so I could lie down for the ride home from the hospital. For weeks, it seemed I was continuously on the edge of a spasm. If I walked on a flat surface it was fine, but any unevenness would cause cramping in my back. When I tried to bend or do housework, I'd feel the warning that a spasm was close. Every time I attempted to do what I used to do, it ended up costing me days of recovery. I was a jogger, and loved to take long walks in the fields, but because of the spasms, I had to stop every kind of physical exercise. Any incline or uneven ground would bring pain. We even had to trade in our car for one that was easier to get in and out of.

Without the emotional lift from exercise, plus chronic pain, depression thundered in, like a lion that had been waiting at my door. Little did I know several more life-altering blows were right around the corner.

Several weeks later, I was making dinner for my family when the phone rang. It was a friend I knew in the small circle of local recording professionals. He was calling to tell me that Larry Ellis, my dear friend who owned the studio where all my music albums had been recorded, had suffered a massive heart attack and died suddenly at age 57.

I froze, realizing Larry had died at the same age as my father. The phone dropped from my hand and I stood speechless, staring out my kitchen window at the leaves falling from the trees in my backyard. There were few people that I cherished like Larry. We'd spent hundreds of hours in his music studio. Without his encouragement, I might never have had the courage to record a single album.

Even though I was in shock, I distinctly remember noticing the azure blue sky that peeked through the trees. It was a picture-perfect fall day, almost as if God was showing off His unfailing banner of love.

"What's the matter?" asked Bill. "Who was that on the phone?"

After a long pause, I whispered, "Larry is dead."

I stood fixated on the leaves out my window. You could actually hear them as they landed—lightly patting the leaves already fallen. They were dropping quickly, as if suddenly being signaled to let go. The long, grey, New York winter was coming, when the sun rarely shines, and the cold goes on forever. It was a foreshadowing of what was ahead, and a prophecy of what would soon be expected of me.

I don't know what to do, God. I was totally in shock. We were almost finished recording my next album—the 11th one he'd produced for me. We'd spend countless hours together, framing each song with accompaniment. Larry was my music mentor, my trusted friend, and a virtual father to me. It was so bizarre that he not only died the same way as my Dad, he died at the same age, too.

One grief seems to stick to another. Often, one loss triggers grief from past losses. Suddenly I was not only grieving Larry, I was remembering the pain of losing my Dad.

Then, as clearly as I've ever heard the Holy Spirit, He said, "You do not know the dips and turns of this dance. Lean in and stay loose." How could this be called a dance? A dance is supposed to be a happy, fun, even thrilling experience. Yet, I'd lost my dear friend, Larry, lost the chance to finish our album and lost the joy of spending time in the studio. I'd lost my Dad, and lost the ability to sit, move, and walk without pain. *How can You call this a dance, God? What does standing on Your shoes look like? How do I apply this on a Monday-Tuesday level?*

Later that evening, I opened my Bible to Psalm 40:17 where David writes, "I am poor and needy ... *yet* ... You think about me."

Are You, Lord? Are You really thinking about me? Where is the peace? Why is this happening? Help me to trust You.

A memory swept over me, bringing the smell of my Dad's cologne to mind. I could envision him in his white dress shirt and shiny black shoes, his strong arms around me as he waltzed around the room. I could no longer hold back the tears. The shock I'd been feeling gave way to heartbroken waves of grief. *Carry me, Lord—I can't dance right now.*

CHAPTER TWELVE

The Meek Shall Inherit Their Mothers

My brother George met a sweet woman at his daily program for adults with special needs, and they married. Their relationship was a match made by the Lord. Our whole family fell in love with Sandy. Mom had done a wonderful job building independence and confidence in George despite his physical challenges. He was ready to be on his own. Their physical and mental disabilities only made them cling closer to each other. They had a wonderful social worker who helped them adjust to independent living.

There was a flip side to this happy event, however. With all three of her children now married and living away from her, my mother was alone in her house for the first time.

During the next year, it became obvious that she'd been depending on George more than any of us realized. She had no one to care for anymore. Mom seemed lost. She was 79 and felt it was time to sell the house and move into an independent living facility.

Helping Mom pack could have been a sitcom. I'd wrap a few things and she'd say, "What's in there?" and unwrap them. So basically, everything got wrapped two or three times. The minute a box was filled, I'd move it out of sight because she'd want to open it again to see inside.

The house sold immediately, and Mom moved into a beautiful senior apartment.

I should have stayed with her the first few nights, but it had only been a couple months since my fall on the stairs, and sleeping on her couch would have been brutal. Still, I wish I'd stayed.

Mom got up in the night, became disorientated, and fell in the bathroom between the commode and the wall. She hit her head and bruised her ribs. The facility wouldn't take her back after her hospital stay, so after consulting with my husband, and my older brother who lived out of state, I moved her into a higher level of care.

We packed again. This time we moved all her furniture and personal things into a storage unit.

The next facility seemed okay on the outside. I was relieved that Mom would finally get the care she needed, but it turned out to be a nightmare. I'll never forget walking into her room and finding Mom slumped over a table with her hair dragging in a bowl of soup. They had insisted that she get out of bed and walk to the table to eat. But her ribs hurt her so much she could barely move. Their excuse for this situation: the state didn't allow eating in bed.

Mom was also drenched in urine. Their excuse: the state didn't allow bedpans.

"She needs a bath," I told an aide. "This is a dignified woman who

always kept herself impeccable. She shouldn't be left like this!"
I bellowed.

I was told there was a bath down the hall, but the state wouldn't allow
them to bathe her—she'd have to do it herself.

I was seething inside. *What kind of place is this? Nobody should be treated
like this.* I felt so guilty, like I wasn't fulfilling my duty, but this was a road
I'd never traveled before. I was raised to let the professionals do their job,
without question. I thought I could trust the staff at this facility; I knew
nothing about the health care system.

Mom and I had always enjoyed a good relationship, but we'd become a
little distant. It's hard to explain why. It wasn't any one thing, but I was busy
with my family and music, and she felt neglected by me after Dad's death. I
wanted to be closer to her, but I didn't know how to bridge the gap.

I helped her to the bath, then helped her undress. I was down on
my knees, trying to get her wet slacks over her feet, when the Lord said,
"This is the way back to your mother's heart."

It takes meekness to serve, to bathe the feet of another. I thought
of the verse in Matthew 5:5 that states the meek shall inherit the earth.
I heard: *The meek shall inherit their mothers.* Tears caught in my throat. His
ways are so simple, so pure-hearted. I got Mom submerged in the tub,
covering her breasts with a towel in respect. She searched my face as I
washed her, and I felt God's presence all around us.

Walls between us began to melt. Every offense harbored in my
heart suddenly seemed insignificant. As I washed her feet, the love I
remembered from long ago trickled up from deep in my heart. I've
never felt such love for my mother as I did at that moment. There was a
tenderness between us that was inexpressible. Our roles had switched as I
took on the mothering. She needed me now.

It was the weekend, and only a small number of staff were on duty. We waited anxiously for mom's pain pill to come. A teenage aide finally came into the room, but she was carrying mom's meds in her bare hand!

"Here's your pain pill, Mrs Fine." Mom reached to take it from her ungloved hand.

"Wait a minute," I said, stopping her. "You're not giving my mother pills straight out of your hand! You've contaminated it." Then I looked at the medicine. "That's not a pain pill."

"Oh, really?" the teen replied, picking it up between her fingers to examine it.

"That's a blood pressure pill. She already had that today. Besides, why would you be dispensing narcotics? You're not qualified to do that."
"Oh-h-h," she said with a confused look, and turned to leave. I followed her straight into the dispensary room and watched her drop the pill from her hand back into a drawer of other pills intended for additional patients.

"Why was my mother soaked with urine?"

"She's supposed to get up and walk to the bathroom, but she won't do it."

"No-oo, she CAN'T do it, she's in pain. Can't somebody help her?"

"We're understaffed on weekends," she replied with a dramatic sigh.

That night, when Mom needed to use the restroom, she tried to walk, stumbled, and fell again.

They called me at midnight to say she was on the way to the hospital in an ambulance.

When I arrived in the emergency room, Mom was totally disoriented, terrified, in pain, and confused. My heart broke. Just a month before, she was taking care of her own home. *What has happened to her, Lord? I should have stayed to help her more.* I could barely breathe with my own back pain. I felt like I was being torn apart.

The hospital finally found another facility that would take her. She'd been treated for the fall, and given more pain meds, but they said there was nothing more they could do. I was thankful for the opening, even though it was a dingy place in the inner city They assured me they would help Mom get back on her feet. The ambulance prepared to take her there, so I told Mom I was going to go home, get a little sleep, and see her in the morning. That was a huge mistake.

The next morning, I took the elevator to the third floor, and when the doors opened, I saw Mom slumped in a wheelchair by the nursing station. When she saw me, her face lit up and she began to weep. "I didn't think I'd ever see you again!" she cried.

"What? Oh Mom, I told you I was coming," I reminded her. She hadn't remembered. She thought that I'd left her alone in that place to die.

I felt like I was totally missing the mark. *I should have known. I should have been more considerate of her needs, not my own.*

Guilt accompanied every step. I didn't know how to manage all the things happening in my life at once.

Mom said she didn't like it there. She said they were "doing things" to her. I got busy finding another place right away. Thankfully, I was able to find an assisted living facility that would take her, one that was much closer to our farmhouse. It seemed perfect. So we began to pack again.

In the meantime, Bill appeared overly exhausted from work and unusually distant, like he'd disappeared into his own world. It wasn't like him. I feared he was getting depressed and because I had my hands full with Mom, I reached out to some men at my church with requests to please visit Bill. They said they would, but no one ever came.

Lord, what is happening? I need my husband! I feel like I'm going to explode with anger for so many reasons. I don't want to be doing this. I want my life back. I want to sit in the fields to look for Your treasures, and soak in Your Word. Why didn't the men come visit Bill? Where is our support system?

I was hopeful Mom would perk up in her new place, maybe even get involved with activities. But she just sat and stared out the window.

"Mom, give it time. You'll adjust, make some new friends. I heard they have a Bridge club here. You love Bridge."

I came back the next day and noticed nothing in her room had been moved. She hadn't opened any of the little packages on her bureau. Mom used to love to putter, but she'd done none of that. She just sat. It looked as if she'd given up. We didn't realize another storm was brewing. The next day, she was rushed to the hospital in excruciating pain. She had a bowel blockage and needed emergency surgery.

The surgery went well, but mom had trouble coming off the support machines. They moved her to intensive care, where she laid for the next 70 days.

"We need to give your mother a peg tube for feeding. Do we have your approval?"

"What's that?" I asked.

"It's a flexible feeding tube placed through the abdominal wall. It will enable us to continue feeding her."

Mom had made it plain in her health care proxy that she didn't want any extreme measures taken. The problem was defining when her treatment went from post-surgical care to long-term chronic care. My older brother lived nearly six hours away in Pennsylvania, but we now spoke often on the phone regarding Mom's care. I agonized over the decision. Without her feeding tube, she wouldn't get her medication. I didn't want to be the one to make that choice.

The next day, when the elevator doors opened on the second floor of the hospital, I was greeted by a nurse, a social worker, and a nun. Thankfully, Bill was with me.

"Mrs. Stevens, we're so sad to tell you that your mother passed just a few minutes ago."

Mysteriously, strength surged through me. I knew the Lord was there. Bill grabbed my elbow. "Sit down, sweetheart," he said.

"I'm okay, honey—really," I said.

I felt a great sense of relief that the decision about the feeding tube had been taken out of my hands. For her sake, I was grateful that her struggle was over. The past four months had been so difficult.

"She went peacefully in her sleep, Mrs Stevens."

"Was anyone with her at the time?"

A young nurse shyly lifted her hand.

"Is this the first time someone has died on your watch?"

She nodded. I wrapped my arms around her and whispered thank you. Her eyes filled with tears.

"Would you like to see her?" she asked us.

Mom was lying peacefully in her bed. The room was cool and quiet. All the machines were gone—just a wilting bouquet of flowers sat next to her glasses on the table beside her bed. Then I noticed she had her shoes on.

"Why is Mom wearing her shoes?"

"She insisted," said the nurse.

"She knew she was going somewhere," added the nun, smiling warmly.

When I'd visited mom the day before, she had been very agitated and kept trying to get up.

"Mom, what are you trying to do?"

"I have to do my housework," she insisted.

I didn't remind her she didn't live at home anymore. "Mom, all your work is done. The house is clean. The laundry is done. The bills are paid, and George is fine."

"Oh ... and who did all that?"

"You did, Mom, and I helped a little."

She smiled and settled down, "Well then, what shall I wear to the wedding?"

I was startled. There was no wedding. George's wedding had been more than a year ago. I wondered if she meant the wedding feast waiting for her in Heaven.

"Why don't you wear that lovely yellow floral?" We spent a little time talking about which outfit would be perfect. Those were the last words we shared.

It was over.

My older brother, Bill, worked for the University of Pittsburgh at Johnstown, but came up to help as often as he could during mom's decline. With each visit, we grew closer and closer, bonding as we hadn't in years. In the middle of so much sadness, I could see God had hidden this bright treasure for me to find—His token of love, sparkling in the darkness.

CHAPTER THIRTEEN

Laughter is Like a Medicine

Sometimes you just have to pause from the intensity and laugh. Bill didn't call me Lucille Ball for nothing. Right in the middle of everything going on, I was "enjoying" the vexatious change of life—for me, a *10-year* transition rivaling an Olympic marathon. According to Dr. James Dobson, a Christian author and psychologist, menopause may take that long in some cases. (I can't wait to ask God about that one!) Bill was graced with enormous, God-breathed, supernatural patience. Handling change—of any kind—has never been my strong suit. I guess I was not the easiest person to live with then.

Bill went so far as to suggest I should wear a red helium balloon on my belt to warn my friends whenever I was "hormonal." He was the only one who thought he was funny.

I've come to the conclusion that God purposely planned for me to live life hard, just to give me plenty of material. Menopause was no exception. I am the voice of every woman too embarrassed to say she feels the same.

"Why do they call it *men*-o-pause? What have men got to do with it?" I beefed. "It's not fair. How many mid-life crises have you had—six, seven? Why do girls get only one?"

"That's because yours lasts 10 years!"

Bill told me the word menopause really should be translated: "*Men ...* O, (you'd better) *pause* (and think before you say anything)."

I was a tad moody, I guess, but it was only because I was sure everyone was ganging up on me. I felt invisible.

"I could drop dead and you wouldn't notice I was even gone until you ran out of clean socks," I whined.

One day as Bill was trying to help me cook dinner, I barked at him, "Why are you doing it THAT way?"

My long-suffering hubby just looked at me and replied, "Who are you? And what have you done with my wife?"

I could become irritable over the silliest things. "Can't you swallow quietly? You sound like you ate a frog." He just picked up the remote and turned up the TV.

I didn't like how my body was changing either. I swear, my boobs dropped a good three inches practically overnight. Luckily, my waist had expanded enough to catch them.

I was either freezing or on fire. We had to buy twin beds because Bill couldn't stand the steam emanating off my body. He tried to cheer me up by making light of things.

"Well, at least we'll save money," he said.

"How?" I answered crisply.

"Easy. We'll stand you in the corner of the living room, and put a fan behind you—you'll heat the entire downstairs."

Again, he was the only one laughing.

The doctor suggested hormone replacement pills, but when she told me weight gain was a side effect, I said no way. "I can already roll down a hill without hitting any bones, why would I want to ingest that stuff?"

I tried to diet. I even joined a weight-loss clinic. But, sadly, I cheated. When the skinny assistant asked me to get on the scale, I held on to the wall!

"Congratulations, Mrs Stevens, you've lost a tenth of a pound this month!"

Guess how much that cost me? It's a miracle I didn't slap her.

I tried jogging again, for two days, that is. That flopped. I joined an exercise group in town, but had to leave because I just couldn't hold back the wise-cracks. I quit before I got kicked out. I tried a low-carb diet and got bored by the third day. That's when I started liking plaques that read: "A balanced diet is a cookie in each hand," or, "I'm not fat—I'm fluffy!"

At least I had a sense of humor ... in retrospect.

Mother always called me her Christian Erma Bombeck. I used to try holding back the humor when I ministered because I thought I was straying from the greater purpose of teaching the Word. Then I realized God was using the stories to bring joy to the Body of Christ.

God has always used laughter in my life. My Dad used to say, "Everything that happens to you in life is just another funny story to tell."

I'll have sudden unexpected bursts of joy that send me into gales of laughter. The Bible says the joy of the Lord is our strength (Nehemiah 8:10), and laughter is like a medicine (Proverbs 17:22), so I decided whenever this happens, I'll just go with it.

Laughter struck one time when I went to visit Bill in the hospital. The poor guy was struggling to pass 12 kidney stones. There was certainly nothing funny happening. I had just parked the car, and had one foot out the door when suddenly I was hit with laughter. It didn't make sense, but for the next 10 or 15 minutes, I dissolved into side-splitting hysterics, tears rolling down my cheeks, while my hoots echoed through the parking garage.

Once I composed myself, I got the other foot out of the car and proceeded into the hospital. God knew I needed an infusion of His strength because when I got to Bill's room, things had suddenly gotten intense. He was having a heart reaction from something they were giving him.

The inner peace I felt was clearly supernatural. I didn't fall apart, cry, become afraid or anxious. There was no doubt in my mind that the laughter I'd experienced beforehand was an infusion of strength straight from the Holy Spirit.

We all know the mood-boosting effects of laughter, but researchers have found humor also strengthens the immune system, boosts energy, diminishes pain, and protects you from the damaging effects of stress. Laughter can also improve the function of blood vessels and increase blood flow, which can protect you against a heart attack or other cardiovascular problems.[1] That's a good reason to laugh everyday.

My grandkids can tell you about my laugh attacks—they've gotten used to them. One day, my seven-year-old grandson William and his friend were having lunch at my house when something tickled my funnybone. Of course, I turned red, and quickly launched from chuckles into full-blown hoots and howls, nearly squeaking as tears streamed down my face. William's friend leaned over and whispered, "What's wrong with your grandma?"

---

1) Robinson, Lawrence, Smith, Melinda, M.S., and Segal, Jeanne, Ph.D., "Laughter is the Best Medicine: The Health Benefits of Humor and Laughter," *Help Guide.Org Trusted guide to mental and emotional help*. Last modified April 2017. Accessed at: http://www.helpguide.org/articles/emotional-health/laughter-is-the-best-medicine.htm

Without hesitation, William responded, "Oh, she just does that."

Over the years, I've learned to see laughter itself as more than just an emotion or experience to share with friends and family. During one service, my pastor spent time pointing out the gifts represented in the congregation. When he came to me, I expected him to say something about my skills as an artist, or a writer, or even a Bible teacher. Instead he said, "And this one has the Lucille Ball thing going on." Everybody laughed, including me.

Although we may not realize it, laughter is actually a gift. Laughter reveals the perspective we hold on life and heralds that God's joy is here.

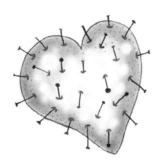

CHAPTER FOURTEEN

A Painful Companion

Back pain continued to be an ongoing problem, but now there was a new dimension to the chronic pain I was experiencing. I'd wake up with burning pain in one leg one day, and the next day, it would be in my arms. Something was always hurting somewhere. My doctor said it was systemic depression. The rheumatologist diagnosed me with a type of fibromyalgia caused by depression. They both recommended anti-depressants.

I was looking forward to relief, but I did not want to take anti-depressants. I wrestled with a sense of embarrassment, even shame. *It's just my imagination. I just need to get my mind off myself,* I thought, knowing what my mom would say. Of course, my father would have insisted, "No little girl of mine gets depressed." He always told me psychiatrists would ruin the world.

I held my prescription for two weeks before I could face handing it in to the pharmacist. Bill was the only one who encouraged me to try it. He watched me struggling against dark moods and pain.

I was still ministering regularly. Not understanding grief, I pushed forward, trying to get my mind off the emotional pain of losing my mom. I began to spend every extra moment I had in my art room. I hadn't taken the time to do art in years because music was my focus. I entered my work in a few art festivals, and did well, but I was having trouble with pain in my hands and neck, so I had to ration my time drawing and painting.

The fibromyalgia began to affect my singing. I'd experience shooting pains up the back of my head and in my jaw. Muscle spasms cramped my tongue and throat, but only when I sang. Slowly it progressed, until it was impossible to sing even one song without having to hold the back of my head.

That was the worst blow of all. I felt like a huge, flourishing tree that had been reduced to a twisted, broken stump. I couldn't take part in praise and worship at church. I couldn't sing my prayers. There was nothing wrong with my vocal chords, just muscle spasms that took every drop of joy out of singing.

Invitations began to taper off. Though I'd always taught the Word when I traveled to minister, music was my strongest calling card. God had used my music as an entrance into denominations that would never have allowed a woman in the pulpit. My songs broke through barriers. I can't count the number of times I'd heard, "You're the first woman we've ever allowed in our pulpit." Music softened hearts and opened doors.

For the next few years, the pain in my head and jaw only worsened. On rare occasions, God would give me a special anointing and I'd sing a song without pain, but the spasms always came back.

I'd never felt so broken. *How could God take this gift away from me? Aren't His gifts everlasting? Had I spoiled something? Become prideful? Taken my gift for granted?* I searched my heart, repented of everything I could think of. Many prayed for me, but nothing improved. *Thirty years, God—did it mean nothing?*

Losing my voice was an enormous loss, but then I learned that after my producer died and his studio was closed, all my music masters were thrown in the trash! Not only did it represent my heart, and the ability to reproduce more CDs, it represented every penny I had ever earned in the ministry. All the money from album sales and speaker honorariums had gone into a savings account for the purpose of producing more music since it took about $10,000 to record and distribute just one album. Over the years, my producer had helped me create 11 full-length recordings.

Perhaps the masters were thrown in the trash because of ignorance, or because the family's grief pushed them to want to remove every trace of the music studio. I'll never know. But for me, it was the nail in the coffin that sealed the end of my music ministry. All the work we had done over 30 years—thrown away like worthless garbage.

Why, Lord? Why wasn't I called? I'm only 30 minutes away, I could have driven there to pick up the masters.

In the beginning, I didn't want to forgive. I felt justified in my anger. I'd been so frugal, saving every penny to record, and to think that more than $100,000 worth of sacrificial investment had been ignorantly discarded was gut-wrenching. It took months of continually giving it to the Lord before I could honestly say it was forgiven. I had to forgive, not once, but over and over and over. I knew unforgiveness would only increase the depression I was already battling. Whenever I pictured my life's work in some dirty dumpster, I had to declare war on that thought and push away every desire to gripe about it. My only hope of moving forward was to hold tightly to the belief that God would redeem this loss—somehow.

My lifeline became "The Lord is near to the brokenhearted and saves those who are crushed in spirit. Many are the afflictions of the righteous, but the Lord delivers him out of them all" (Psalm 34:18, NIV).

The last hope that I would ever minister in music again was laid in the ground, buried forever. It was time to embrace a new season. In the process of adjusting to the loss of my voice, I made an important discovery. My true gift was not music—it was creativity.

I began to focus on other areas of creativity. I pulled out some old sketches I'd started for several children's books. Then, with Bill's encouragement, I took a huge leap of faith and went to a Christian writer's conference. I wasn't even sure that I could write. Being surrounded by seasoned writers was intimidating, and I found my thoughts returning to the confidence I'd known with music. *Lord, did all that dedication and expense mean anything? If it was You, why did it die? Was it just a vain imagination?*

Fresh tears of surrender flowed down my face as I once again grieved the loss of my voice. "You will deliver me out of them all," I whispered as I fell asleep. The next day at the conference, after a lecture on building strong characters, the class went for refreshments. Two women were standing close by, so I introduced myself.

"What type of writing environment do you prefer?" I asked

One of them said, "I have to have total silence."

The other woman chimed in, "I listen to Christian music, but there are only two specific artists I listen to. One, uh, I can't remember her name ... well, anyway ... and the other one is Marji Stevens."

I almost dropped my cup. "I'm Marji Stevens."

She stared at me blankly and said, "Ohhh, how interesting you have the same name. This Marji Stevens is famous. She's recorded a bunch of albums."

Famous? That sure seemed odd to hear connected to my name. "Uh-h-h, yes, I've recorded."

"Noooo," she chuckled, "this is THE Marji Stevens."

"What's your favorite song?" I asked. When I recited the lyrics, her jaw dropped, but then she blinked and changed the subject.

She couldn't believe it was me. I dropped the subject, because I knew it wasn't about her recognizing me; it was God showing me that my music was still blessing people even though I wasn't singing. *My fruit remains*, He whispered to my heart.

As if a sign that God could bring new life from what felt like ashes, the piece of writing I'd submitted won the "most promising new writer" award at the conference! I went home with a new sense of purpose. *Music was a season*, I thought. *Writing will be my new adventure.*

CHAPTER FIFTEEN

Bernice

Bill's Dad passed away in the early '80s, and for 15 years, his mother, Bernice, lived alone. She seemed to be doing alright, or so we thought. But we began to notice that she rocked back and forth when she sat, as if she was trying to get her stationary chair to move.

"Ma, why are you rocking?" Bill asked.

She seemed a bit disarmed by his question, then she stiffened her back and announced, "I am NOT rocking!" End of discussion. That topic was now off limits.

We were told that the rocking could be a type of self-soothing from being so isolated. She never told us that she wasn't driving as frequently, or getting out to see her friends. In addition, several of her friends had recently passed away. We were concerned but didn't quite know how to approach the subject of moving. We knew it was time for new living arrangements, but how do you tell a ferociously independent, strong-willed, extremely private person—one determined never to be a "bother"—that she had to give up her home?

"I'd rather be dead than go into a nursing home," she said in a huff, folding her arms over her chest.

God was preparing all of us for a major change.

"She can move in with us," Bill told me privately.

"You've got to be kidding," I barked. "That will never work."

Though my words sounded firm, my heart was whispering another message. I dreaded the thought of what God might be asking. We'd always had a polite, but tense relationship. Living together? Impossible.

I was supposed to pick her up and take her for her annual physical one day when she called and asked me to cancel the appointment.

"I'm too sick to my stomach to go. Will you call for me, please?" This was totally out of character. When I hung up, I felt a definite uneasiness in my spirit, and called the doctor's office to say I was bringing her in, but not for a physical. I never called her back to say we were coming to pick her up, because we knew she'd resist. We just showed up.

Bernice was in the middle of having a heart attack. If I'd waited for her approval, she would have died. She got to the hospital just in time. The doctor said open-heart surgery would be needed. Even though she was 82 years old, he was confident she'd come through and be "ready to dance on New Year's Eve."

Her stubborn resolve now proved to be her greatest asset. The recovery was intensive, long, and difficult. Bill and I told her she could live with us until she got her strength back. We hoped it would give us time to approach the subject of making it permanent. In the meantime, she stayed in a little bedroom off the kitchen—right in the middle of everything. I knew that would be too difficult on everyone, so we all agreed to put her house on the market and build an in-law apartment at the far end of our farmhouse so we could each have our own space.

Our relationship had sweetened over the years, and I could tell—
though she would never admit it—she really needed our help. Bill and I
were in total agreement that this was what the Lord wanted us to do.

After Bernice moved in, all her rocking stopped. She held her head
straighter, and she seemed really happy. There was a lot of activity in our
home, and she had her beloved son nearby. Bill drove her to doctor's
appointments and grocery shopping. My job remained the same it had
always been—sit and talk.

"Two women in the same house will never work," she told me one
afternoon over coffee.

I became increasingly aware that many of her statements were really
questions. *Will this arrangement work? Am I a bother?*

When our last dog died, I was not interested in getting another dog.
I'd made it clear to Bill I was tired of all the dog hair. However, God had
other plans.

"I think we ought to buy Bamma a little dog," I told Bill at breakfast
after church.

"But I thought you said no more dogs ... " Bill had his I'm-going-to-
get-my-way grin on his face. He was quite in awe that I'd changed my mind.

"I know what I said, but the Lord keeps nudging me that Bamma
needs a little fluff-ball puppy to love."

Bill laughed. "God told me the same thing in church, but I didn't
know how to tell you!"

We finished our meal hanging over the newspaper and found an ad
for Shih Tzu puppies. We drove about an hour to a farm and there she
was—Molly. She was the runt of the litter and couldn't even get over the
doorstep to greet us. "That's the one," Bill said, scooping her up in his

hands. She started licking him immediately. When I tried to hold her, she nipped my nose. *Oh dear, what does this mean?* I thought. But Bill was sold. On the way home, she tinkled on my church slacks.

When we pulled into our driveway, Bamma was sitting on the front porch. When I emerged from the car holding Molly, I wished I had a movie of Bamma's reaction.

"CAREFUL, Marjorie, you'll hurt her!"

I put Molly in her arms and it was one of the only times I saw tears in her eyes.

Molly became the queen of the house. I was quickly displaced. Now Bamma had a purpose—and a focus—for all her love. I've always joked that the only reason Bamma lived to be 97 was because she didn't believe I'd take care of the dog properly.

"You have to feed her, Marjorie."

"Everyday?" I kidded.

Bamma had her chair, and Molly had one, too.

As Bamma aged, she started transferring her feelings onto the dog. If she was lonely, she'd say, "Molly needs more attention. Look how lonely she is." If I was gone several hours she'd say, "Molly missed you. She's frightened when you leave." Bamma never admitted any weakness, so this was her way of letting me know what she needed. The Lord gave me this insight, so I stopped being annoyed by it, and started listening more carefully.

"Molly is bored. Look how she just hangs in the window looking out." Bamma spent her days sitting in her chair looking out the window. She always insisted she was fine, but I knew she had to get a little bored once in awhile.

I took the cue, "Why don't we go out to lunch?"

"That would be lovely, Marjorie. Only if you will let me pay, of course. I'll get a fat-free turkey sandwich without mayonnaise." She ate that every day.

Guess what? Molly wasn't bored anymore.

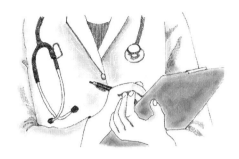

CHAPTER SIXTEEN

The Diagnosis

Bill was in his 30th year of teaching high school when he began having trouble with his breathing. It was almost impossible for him to lecture without becoming breathless. He was tired all the time and seemed to be battling depression, which was not like him. The breathing difficulties had him worried—very worried, but, like his mother, he never admitted it. He held everything inside. That year, his high school offered an early retirement package. Bill had a list of things that he asked God to confirm first, before he would consider it. Every step lined up, and Bill retired from teaching.

Bill had never been able to travel with me, but now he could—and he wanted to. It was a dream come true. Finally, we were a team in ministry. He would take care of the book table and pray. He also ministered to the men. We traveled frequently for about a year when Bill began to have trouble with his breathing again. We attributed it to allergies or coming down with a cold. He got worse.

Gradually, Bill started to excuse himself from meetings to go back to our room to sleep. He said the women's perfume, powder, and hairspray bothered him. Then his sensitivities went a step further. If he ate anything too hot, or too cold, too spicy, salty or sweet, his throat would close as his larynx would spasm. He had an attack during a conference dinner and it was deeply embarrassing. For a man who didn't like any attention drawn to him, he decided it was best to stop traveling and stay home.

The Lord knew how much I loved to minister, so I believe He made it easier for me to sit tight by slowly reducing the number of invitations I received. I worried it was because I wasn't singing, but the Lord let me know He just wanted me to stay closer to home.

The doctors diagnosed Bill with severe reflux, but they couldn't explain his exhaustion and continued breathing problems. When he later developed kidney stones and went into the hospital, the doctors discerned something else was going on and started extensive testing.

The doctor told us, "Bill, you have a condition called sarcoidosis. It can affect any organ in the body, but yours is surrounding your lungs and esophagus. Not to worry, though, we can manage the symptoms with medicine."

They prescribed steroids, and initially, Bill felt much better. He had more energy, and his breathing improved as the inflammation subsided. It seemed miraculous.

However, steroids have some nasty side effects, so the doctor wanted Bill to get off them as soon as possible.

For the next two years, Bill was on and off steroids multiple times. Each time, the prescription strength increased. Getting off the medicine became increasingly difficult. Bill's face became swollen and his vision began to blur.

"Prednisone is like fertilizer for cataracts, but you can't have eye surgery until you get your blood pressure up," the doctor warned.

Bamma hovered over Bill. I could see God's wisdom in having her live with us. The long drive back and forth to her house would have made it difficult for them to get together, and exhausting for me. Here, she could be with her son everyday.

"Marjorie, Bill looks pale. What does the doctor say?"

It must have been very hard for her to stand back and let me care for him my way. I tried to keep her abreast of every detail, but she wanted more information than I could provide.

"Are you feeding him? ... Can I buy some ice cream? You'd have to go get it, but I'll pay ... Should I make some soup?"

"Of course I'm feeding him, Bamma. I figured out years ago he wants to eat every day—like the dog." She didn't understand or appreciate my sarcasm.

I said no to the soup, but she made it anyway. I'll never forget the sight of her standing at the kitchen counter carefully washing and rewashing the vegetables, then chopping them into tiny pieces.

"They have to be small because he can choke," she volunteered over her shoulder. Each piece was bathed with her loving, protective care.

"He shouldn't eat salt—it will drive his blood pressure up," she warned.

"But the doctor said he needs to eat lots of salt because his blood pressure is too low."

She looked puzzled. "It is? When did this happen?"

I'd told her twice before, but she didn't remember.

"My sister was a nurse, you know."

"Yes, I know."

We seemed to compete about who had the best advice when it came to Bill's health. She loved to shower any weakness with instant

89

tomato soup or sweets. I wanted to eliminate sugar and preservatives, and add plenty of vitamins. Everything was measured against what she'd heard her sister say, but her sister would have been more than 100 years old by then. I finally invited Bamma to come with us to the doctor's appointment so she could ask him all the questions she wanted. She said it was none of her business.

My stamina was wearing thin. It was so sad to see Bill's interests falling away one by one. He'd try to target shoot, and do pottery, but it was too strenuous. He was constantly tired. I'll never forget the day he almost drove the car into a ditch. When we got home, he handed me the car keys. He was silent for days after this. It was the battle of his lifetime, as he wrestled against increasing fragility.

Now it was my job to take Bamma to her appointments and to get groceries. I really didn't mind, but I wasn't comfortable leaving him home alone. He could walk around and do a few things for himself, but his blood pressure was starting to drop unexpectedly, and when it did, he'd fall. One time, he fell against the bathroom sink and broke his rib. The job of caring for Bill was too big for one person, so I enlisted the help of the family on a more regular basis.

I continued taking Bamma for groceries. My already stretched patience was tested every time we got in the car.

"Marjorie, you have to stop at the stop sign."

In the beginning, I would fume, or make a wisecrack. Then I realized I was adding to my own stress by being defensive.

"Marjorie, you're going to get us killed!"

"Bamma, I've never run a stop sign and never had an accident. Can't you relax and trust me?"

"We'd better get home," she countered. "Molly must be getting nervous."

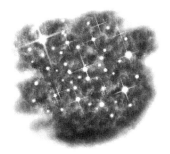

CHAPTER SEVENTEEN

A Touch of Blue

I was working at my desk one afternoon when a sudden uneasiness rose in my spirit. I knew I had to go check on Bill napping upstairs. As I stood up, Bamma came around the corner.

"Marj, will you go check on Bill? He's been sleeping an awfully long time."

"Yes, actually I was just about to," I said. She must have had the same sense that something was wrong.

Bamma had been with us for about five years. She was 90 years old and though healthy, she was growing more unsteady on her feet.

"I'd go check on him myself," she apologized. "But I can't climb those steep stairs."

"No worries, I'm going," I replied over my shoulder as I started up the stairs. "I'm sure he's fine."

The bedroom was at the end of a narrow hallway. The ceilings upstairs were low and everything was uneven. It was mid-afternoon and I could see the sunlight streaming into the bedroom windows.

My stomach instantly knotted with fear when I saw Bill. He was lying on his back in bed with his mouth open. He looked grey. I reached for his hand and it was ice cold. I called his name loudly and shook his shoulders, but he didn't respond.

Shaking, I grabbed the phone beside his bed and dialed 911. I tried pushing on his chest, but I didn't know CPR. I heard the alarm go off at the fire station in town. Then I phoned my son who was farming the property next door. I was relieved when I heard his voice.

"Kyle, come quick! I can't wake your father."

I hated to leave Bill's side, but I had to unlock the door for the ambulance crew.

"What's happening?" Bamma asked as she grabbed onto the counter. I raced past her to open the door.

"The ambulance is coming. I need you to take the dog into your apartment. They told me to secure any animals."

"What's wrong?" She was pale and I could see the terror in her eyes.

"I'm having a little trouble waking Bill." I tried not to alarm her, and I didn't have any time to explain.

Just then, Kyle burst in the kitchen door and ran up the stairs. I followed him, calling out the details.

"Dad?" Kyle touched Bill's foot. "Dad?" Then he ran his fingernails over the arches of Bill's feet. I knew why. Bill had no tolerance for his feet being touched. Even if he was asleep, he would recoil. This time he didn't move, not even a twitch.

We froze. Neither of us wanted to be the first to say it: Bill was gone.

I was gripped with a force so strong, I was almost paralyzed. I couldn't react. I couldn't cry. I couldn't think. I just stood there staring at Bill.

The sound of the ambulance grew louder and louder. This time, it didn't pass our house on its way to a nameless emergency. This time, it wasn't someone else's tragedy—it was *ours*. It was coming to *our* house. I turned to sit down. Kyle remained by Bill's bed. Just as we heard the sound of the ambulance crew coming up the stairs, Bill suddenly spoke!

"Mimmy, I've just seen Heaven."

Kyle and I looked at each other in shock. Bill opened his eyes. "I've just seen Heaven." Then he lifted himself up on one elbow and smiled at me.

I walked over to the side of his bed. The space was too narrow for a chair and I didn't want to crowd him on the bed. I squeezed his arm and leaned against the wall.

"I heard you calling my name. I could see you pounding on my chest, but I saw you from somewhere way up there." He motioned with his hand, indicating that it was higher than the ceiling.

"You heard me?"

"I couldn't answer you. I wanted to, but I wasn't *here*, I was ... " The ambulance crew struggled to carry the stretcher up the narrow stairway, and almost couldn't make it fit around the corner. Four men came in the room, leaving the stretcher in the hallway.

"Mr. Stevens, what's going on?" asked the EMT as he opened his medical case.

"I don't know exactly, but I'm fine now," Bill answered.

"He's NOT fine!" I blurted out, beginning to cry. Kyle put his arm around me to steady me. "He was completely unresponsive, cold, and grey, just a minute ago! Ask my son, he'll tell you. He was gone!"

Kyle nodded his head. "I'm fairly certain, guys, he was totally unresponsive."

"But I'm fine now," Bill said with a wide grin.

"Well, let's have a listen." The EMT took out his stethoscope and opened Bill's shirt. "There has definitely been some activity with your heart. We'll take you to the hospital and let them sort this out."

"There's really no need for that," Bill insisted.

"You can't be fine!" I cried. "You have to go to the hospital and let them find out what just happened to you."

But Bill wouldn't go. "Really, trust me. I *know* I'm fine."

The EMT made him sign a release form. Kyle shook hands with the men, and I escorted them to the door.

"Thank you for coming. I wish he'd go. What should I do?" I asked.

"Well," said the EMT, "it might be a good idea to take him to be checked by his primary doctor, just to be safe."

I thanked them again and closed the door, then went to check on Bill's mom.

I walked softly into her apartment. Bernice didn't look up as usual. She just sat in her chair with her head bowed, her rosary beads dangling from her hand. She suddenly seemed so old. The skin on her hands was paper thin. She looked terribly frail. Her shoulders drooped, her shiny, silver hair was thinning. When she realized I'd stepped into the room, she tucked her rosary under her sweater, but didn't look up.

"Mom, Bill is okay. I couldn't wake him up before. I didn't know if he was in a coma or if it was more serious. He woke up right before the ambulance got here. Even Kyle tried to wake him and couldn't. They checked him thoroughly, but Bill didn't want to go to the hospital. So, I'll take him to his regular doctor in the next few days. Bill told me to tell you he's okay, and he'll try to come downstairs in a little while to talk. Do you want to try going upstairs?"

She shook her head, and didn't answer. Her face was ashen and I could tell she'd been crying. Bernice was a person who rarely showed any emotion. I wished she could have maneuvered our steep stairs to see Bill for herself, but at 90 years old she avoided steps completely.

"I promise I'll come back soon and tell you all the details. Just watch Molly, okay?" The dog looked up when she heard her name. "She's probably very frightened."

Bamma tucked her long, thin fingers around Molly's side and said, "There, there, baby, it's all right now. You're all right."

Bernice lived for her only son, and her little Shih Tzu. I hoped having to focus on the dog would help her while she waited for Bill.

Kyle and Bill were talking when I returned. When Bill saw me he held out his hand, "Mimmy, I'm sorry I frightened you, I saw you pushing on my chest, and I heard you, but I couldn't respond." He frowned, unable to find the words to explain, then he squeezed my hand.

For the next two hours, Kyle and I listened as Bill told us what he experienced.

"I didn't actually see the Lord," he said, "but I felt the heat of His cheek close to mine, like this ... " Bill put the flat of his hand a half inch away from the side of his face. "And He whispered, 'Fear not.'"

Bill closed his eyes and for a moment seemed to drift off, as if he was in and out of consciousness. We waited several minutes before he could continue.

"I was taken through some kind of portal, or opening. That's when I saw the most amazing sight stretched out in every direction. A sky ... uh, I think it was a sky ... it was the most incredible kind of blue. Not a royal blue, or baby blue—it wasn't navy, it was similar to an August azure sky, yet totally different. I've never seen this blue before. It also held millions of lights that looked like stars, but they were different from stars, and they stretched out as far as I could see in every direction."

Again, he drifted off, as if what he'd experienced was now the greater reality, and he wanted to return.

He opened his eyes again and continued, "We don't have adequate language to describe what I saw."

"Did the Lord say anything to you?" I asked.

"Yes, He said I had to go back because it wasn't my time yet, and because you weren't ready to be a widow."

I was stunned. *I wasn't ready? Was that a good thing, or a bad thing?*

I didn't know how to react to that. Had my husband been in the presence of Jesus in Heaven, and was told to leave because I wasn't ready?

My mind whirled with questions. *Was this true? Why did God say that? How can I ever be 'ready' to lose the love of my life? Did He send Bill back just to help me get ready?*

Bill took a sip of water. He closed his eyes for a moment, then continued. "I've always believed that God knows even the most intimate things about me, but now I deeply know it. He allowed me to have this experience because He knew exactly what I needed. He knew my thoughts without me having to speak. We had wordless communication."

He took another sip of water. "In my thoughts, I was questioning my struggle with ... you know." Bill looked at me. I nodded. He didn't want to voice the issue in front of his son. I knew about it because we had no secrets. Bill cleared his throat and continued.

"I didn't have to verbalize my thoughts. The Lord knew what I was thinking. Instantly, I was in another place, a room ... or a cave ... I don't know. I saw a large figure towering in front of me. I couldn't see his face, but I knew it was Jesus. Laid across my feet was a heavy metal chain. I knew it represented sin. Then I saw a single drop of blood fall from the Lord's hand. When the blood touched the heavy links of the

96

chain, it instantly dissolved, as if the chain was made of paper. Then, it completely vanished."

Bill closed his eyes and paused for several minutes. Tears slipped from the corner of his eyes. He was not a man inclined to cry. He took a deep breath and cleared his throat. "The chain was gone! I saw it disappear with my own eyes. The power of His blood dissolved my sin." He looked at me. "Sin is powerless before the blood of Christ."

There was a hush in the room. I sensed the presence of the Lord. It felt as if each molecule of air had suddenly become pregnant with life. Undeniably, it was the Holy Spirit descending to confirm what Bill was saying.

Kyle and I both lost track of time as we listened to Bill. Then the Lord reminded me that poor Bernice was downstairs waiting to hear more about what was happening. I had to tear myself away.

"I've got to check on Bamma. I'll be back, okay?"

"Tell her I'm fine, but don't tell her anything else. She'll be more receptive if it comes from me."

As I walked down the stairs, I prayed that the Lord would free me from every chain, every bondage holding me back from the fullness of life. I knew I needed to find more time to be in His presence. I knew I had resentment in my heart towards Bill's mother. I needed more of God's love, more understanding, more patience, more of Him.

Bernice had dozed off in her armchair. An empty mug of instant tomato soup was on the table next to her. When Molly got up to greet me, Bernice woke up.

"How is my son?"

"He's doing fine. He and Kyle are still talking. Bill told me to tell you he'll come downstairs later and talk to you."

"What happened?" she persisted.

"I don't understand it all. Bill wants to tell you himself. At least, I'm happy to say, the EMT said he is not in any danger. I hope to take him to the doctor tomorrow."

"Molly was sick with worry," she said. "She thought she was going to lose him. I don't think she could survive that."

I didn't have the heart to tell her the way I'd found Bill. I didn't know how much he wanted her to know, except that he was fine now. It was his story to tell.

CHAPTER EIGHTEEN

Bad Drops

Bill agreed to see the doctor the next day. His regular doctor was traveling, so we saw Dr. Ness instead. They always let us come in the emergency entrance to avoid the waiting room congestion, and avoid any possible exposure to illnesses. Bill was too weak to be exposed to crowds. I dropped him off right by the door and he hurried in to find a seat before his blood pressure began to drop. I parked and dashed in through the primary entrance to check him in. They let me go into the examining room and wait with Bill. I found him sitting on a chair, bent over, with his head between his knees.

"Are you okay?" I asked. I'd seen Bill in this pose multiple times. I'd hoped never to see it again after he'd been with Jesus.

"Bad drop ... " he managed to say. It sometimes took a full 10 minutes for his blood pressure to rise again.

Part of Bill's condition was severe orthostatic hypotension. When he stood to walk, his blood pressure would drop drastically. Often, he'd be on the edge of blacking out. His ears would start to ring loudly and he'd temporarily lose his sight. Most mornings he started the day with extreme nausea and vomiting. He could no longer hope to drive, and walking more than 20 or 30 feet brought on an attack. When he was sitting down, his blood pressure would return to normal and he seemed fine. We never learned what was causing this condition.

There was a soft knock at the door and the doctor walked in and shook Bill's hand. "What's happening?" he asked, nodding a hello my way.

Dr. Ness was the epitome of softness. He talked softly and slowly; even his movements were soft.

"I found Bill cold and unresponsive. Our son Kyle was there. We both tried to wake him but he was gone ... *dead*," I said dramatically.

The doctor picked up his stethoscope without responding, and calmly took his time listening to Bill's heart. Then he pulled up a chair and sat down.

"Bill, why don't you tell me what happened."

Bill told him the entire story, including what he saw in Heaven, and that the Lord had sent him back because I wasn't ready to be a widow. The doctor glanced back at me and smiled.

Dr. Ness listened carefully to all the details of his experience, then without saying anything, he stood again and listened to Bill's lungs.

"What do you think?" I asked. "I really thought he should be checked because what if something did happen that could have been prevented if we'd known how to avoid it."

Dr. Ness looked at me and nodded. His expression was warm and it reassured me that I'd done the right thing.

He sat down again, and we waited for his response. Silence fell over the room. I fidgeted. Bill closed his eyes.

"Well," he said calmly. "I believe you have had a classic near-death experience, Bill." He paused again for a long time, "What a blessing."

"Is this going to happen again?" I asked. "It was so frightening."

"I'm sure it was," he replied, raising his eyebrows. "And a blessing at the same time, right? I don't know if it will happen again—that's in God's hands. Bill, your heart sounds fine, but your lungs tell me you need to stay on your oxygen for the sarcoidosis. I can see no reason why you can't go home and continue with the things you were able to do before this event."

"But why did this happen? Should he see the specialist again, or go to the hospital for more tests?" I protested. The two of them sat there so peaceful. I wasn't satisfied.

"You can see your specialist if you wish. I can't tell you why this happened and, no, I don't think Bill needs to go to the hospital."

Bill stood up, thanked the doctor, and hurried down the hall to find a chair by the emergency door before his blood pressure dropped. Frustration knotted in my stomach. Dr. Ness could read me well. When Bill was gone, he patted me on the shoulder, "I know," he said. "This is very tough." Tears instantly burst from my eyes. He didn't question my concern. "Let's just see what happens. You can call me anytime."

I pulled the car up and helped Bill get in. He was worn out. Again, his blood pressure dropped dangerously low. When he was able to speak, Bill reached over and patted my shoulder just like Dr. Ness. "Feel better now?"

"Yes, I do. I'm glad we went."

When we pulled in the driveway, Bernice and Molly were standing at the window.

"What did the doctor say?" she asked as Bill rushed in, looking for the nearest chair. Bill couldn't answer. He put his head between his knees and worked at breathing. I turned the oxygen up on his machine. Finally, he recovered.

"Ma, I'm fine. My heart is okay. I didn't have a heart attack. I just need to stay on the oxygen as before. Don't worry."

She looked over Bill's head and caught my eye. "*Is* he okay, Marj?" I shrugged and caught her gaze. I couldn't say he was fine because nothing was fine. I knew he was trying to console his mom, but Bernice and I knew things were getting worse. Telling Bernice not to worry about her only child was like trying to defy gravity.

As I left to make Bill's lunch, I heard him say, "Ma, have you ever heard about someone having a near-death experience?" He felt it was finally time to tell her the rest of his story.

They talked for a long time. I only interrupted to bring him some soup. Bernice's empty mug was next to her chair, so I knew she'd had her usual instant tomato soup. Then I left the room.

I went to the couch and lied down. I kept picturing that empty mug next to Bamma's chair. She was such a creature of habit. She had one favorite mug she used for coffee in the morning, tea in the afternoon, and tomato soup in between. Occasionally, I'd offer to wash it because I wondered if she was able to see how gross it was. Her response was always the same. "No, Marjorie, you'll use soap and ruin it."

Mother's Day, holidays, and birthdays brought a plethora of new mugs. The whole family was trying to get her to switch. But every new mug would end up in the cupboard, unused.

My family used to bark at me "Geesh, Mom, why don't you wash Bamma's mug for her?" I gave up trying to explain. It would have been nice just to clear my reputation, but Bernice wouldn't let me near it. I knew their conversation about visiting Heaven was way outside her comfort zone. She'd have to change her 90-year-old firm and unyielding belief system.

In the days ahead, while Bernice and I rankled over the little things, like her tomato soup-crusted mug, Bill was entertaining guests who came to hear about his near-death experience. We'd only told a few close friends, but the word spread like wildfire. We started getting phone calls from people we normally had no contact with. One noticeable guest was a young college student whom we'd hired to seal our driveway. Bill met him on the porch with his oxygen tank. "Hey there, can you sit a minute? I've got an amazing story to tell you." They talked for more than two hours. As it turned out, the young man had fallen away from the Lord. He was visibly impacted by Bill's testimony and returned several times to visit.

The presence of the Lord was all around Bill, and he loved sharing his story with everyone he saw. It made me think of what the council of elders said about Peter and John: though they were just ordinary men, "they were astonished at their courage and took note that these men had been with Jesus" (Acts 4:13, NIV).

CHAPTER NINETEEN

How Long Do I Have?

Bill's symptoms seemed manageable for a long time, until he contracted pneumonia. His occasional use of oxygen quickly became a daily need.

After months of being sick, it was evident Bill wasn't getting better. We returned to the lung specialist for more tests. He always wanted me to go into the examining room as another set of ears. The long walk down the corridor from the waiting room was difficult. The doctor was waiting by the door and quietly observed what happened. Bill was not only struggling to breathe, his blood pressure was becoming the bigger problem. I was grateful that the doctor could witness it for himself.

After the doctor finished his exam, Bill leaned forward and looked him in the eyes. "Doc, I want you to be straight with me. How much time do I have?"

My mind whirled. *Why would Bill ask that? This is just a flare-up. The doctor just needs to boost his steroids and he'll get better just like before,* I thought. I wasn't sure I wanted to know the doctor's answer. Fear knotted in my stomach and everything felt surreal. *We'll pull out of this—don't we always?*

The doctor was clearly uncomfortable being put on the spot. He put his head down and fidgeted for several minutes.

"Bill, I believe you could easily live another five years if you don't contract pneumonia again."

We were stunned speechless. *Five years? Bill could die in only five years? This can't be true.*

Bill waited on a bench outside the office while I got the car. I didn't want to cry, but tears caught in my throat, and spilled down my cheek. We drove home in silence, but before we went in the house Bill said, "I don't want you to tell my mother what the doctor said. She's too frail."

"Okay, I won't." I knew she'd be asking me for every detail. The news was so heavy on my heart, I prayed the words would not come tumbling out.

The next few days Bill kept to himself. I frequently asked how he was, but he only answered, "How do you think?" I tried to give him as much space as possible, but I longed to connect. Finally, almost a week later, he opened up.

"If I don't get better, I'll never be able to teach my grandkids how to hunt and shoot a bow. I won't get to take them fishing or teach them how to throw clay on the wheel. And I promised to take them to Disney World."

Heavy sadness hung over our home. It was so difficult to pray, or think clearly. Between caring for Bamma, communicating with the family, dealing with chronic pain, and encouraging Bill, I was exhausted.

My neighbor, Coleen, a nurse, was an enormous strength during this time. I went to her with all my medical questions. She'd helped me through my mother's hospitalization and passing, now she was helping me with Bill. She kept reminding me to take care of myself.

Bill slept constantly, and when he was awake, he was tethered to an oxygen machine by a 50-foot tube.

"This is not what I'd planned for your future," he said. His eyes were soft and filled with tears as he reached out and touched my cheek.

I couldn't respond at first. He was the one so sick, and yet he was still caring for me and trying to protect me.

"Honey, my future is in God's hands," I said. "He has a hope and a future for me. Right now, I wouldn't want to be anywhere else but here with you. The doctors really can't tell us how long you have," I whispered.

"Yeah, I know," he sighed.

Bill often asked me to lay hands on him and pray. Each time we approached the Lord together, the tangible presence of God would become so evident. God filled us with peace and the reassurance that we were in the palm of His hands. These were the moments when I felt the closest to my husband.

"Do you think we should try going to the Cleveland Clinic or to Boston?" I asked.

"No more tests," he said.

Bill was tired of doctors and hospitals. I feared he was giving up. I felt powerless, as if I had no say in what was happening in my life. The sadness was stifling. I wanted him to fight, to try everything, but he wouldn't. He was fading away, getting weaker and weaker.

While Bill was sleeping, I drifted into Bamma's apartment, hoping for some encouragement.

"Why won't he fight? He's giving up! He's depressed and he won't talk to anyone. I'm trying to help him, but ..."

"He's *sick,* Marjorie," she answered in a demeaning tone, as if I didn't get it.

"I *know* that! But you don't just give up. You have to try everything, keep fighting," I insisted. "Right?"

"*You* can't change him," she said sternly. "This is what he wants and you have to accept it. By the way, did you feed him today?"

"Seriously?" I nipped.

She didn't appreciate my tone of voice. She just stiffened her back and set her gaze out the window. I left the room.

I didn't want to have to explain everything to my mother-in-law. Just once, I wanted her to agree with me. I wanted her to tell me I was doing a great job caring for Bill, and that Bill was lucky to have me. I was already exhausted, feeling defeated and insignificant, and now my mother-in-law overwhelmed my home with her constant questions. Just once, I wanted to feel as though I didn't have to defend myself. Her constant, corrective tone reinforced all my old feelings that she never did approve of me, that I wasn't capable without her constant instruction, and that I'd never be good enough for her son.

Emotionally, I had nothing left. I couldn't be nice. I didn't even want to *try* to be nice. I resented her presence in the middle of everything. Everyday, I was swallowing more and more anger, fighting to hold my tongue.

Why is this happening to us? Why aren't You doing anything to fix it? I'm tired of asking and asking, and I'm tired of the constant emotional fight.

CHAPTER TWENTY

Listen for His Heartbeat

My escape was the art corner I'd set up in the garage. I went there every spare moment. A baby monitor kept me in touch with Bill and Bamma. If all I got was a half hour, it helped me survive the tension.

Bill could no longer go to church. It was too risky with a compromised immune system. Eventually, I stopped going too.

At times, I felt guilty about my spiritual life. My prayer time was too often a wordless meltdown, or I'd fall asleep, or get interrupted. I felt as if I was losing touch with the Lord.

A few girlfriends were concerned that I wasn't in church and came to persuade me that I needed to attend their Bible study. When I declined politely, they argued with me.

"This will be good for you. We've seen ... well, we've noticed ... you need this."

I had no reserve. I knew they meant well, but I hadn't seen either one of them for almost a year. Now that they were starting up a Bible study, they were suddenly interested in me. They kept pressuring. Finally, I lost my temper.

"The last thing I need is to be with a bunch of chatty girls with their happy smiles and have to fake it. I don't need a Bible study, I need a sincere friend who will come sit with me, and let me complain about how much I hate my life right now. The cold, hard facts are that I'm losing my husband and I'm responsible for a 90-year-old mother-in-law who doesn't trust me. I don't need a lecture on praising the Lord or declaring the right verse—I need someone to cry with."

They stared at me. "God is good, all the time," one said.

"He doesn't give us more than we can handle," said the other.

"So you say—but it sure feels like it, and you're not helping."

They left, and neither one returned to be that friend.

The days dragged on. Sadness ruled my heart. My quiet time was nonexistent and I felt farther from the Lord than ever before.

"Father, I can't see Your face," I cried. "I'm in such a dark place, and I feel so restricted."

Suddenly, a cartoon picture appeared in my mind. A large, fluffy mother hen was sitting in her nest with one wing neatly folded at her side. The other wing was puffed out and I could see two little chicken feet sticking out from the bottom.

The little chick peeped, "I can't see my mother's face! It's dark, and I feel restricted."

Then a caption appeared along the bottom of the scene. When you can't see your Father's face, listen for His heartbeat.

I quickly grabbed a piece of paper and sketched what I saw. The little chick couldn't have been any closer to its mother. She was holding it tight and snug under her wing. That's why it seemed so dark. The shade of her wing was blocking the natural light.

Joy trickled into my heart. God knew my circumstances. It wasn't time for me to be running around. He was holding me against His breast, protecting me like a mother hen. This was not the time to grade myself over spiritual disciplines. It was time to snuggle close, rest, trust, and listen for His heartbeat.

Little did I know the life-changing events that were soon to take place. Little did I know so many of the Lord's encouragements over the years would come flooding back to minister to me again and again.

He continuously reassured me that I was tucked under the unfailing wing of the Almighty. I'd been judging the reality of His love by my behavior. When I was seeking Him, and reading the Word, I felt loved. When I didn't get angry or hold any grudges, I felt loved. But when I didn't have the time and reacted poorly to my surroundings, I imagined He was withholding His love. My limited understanding of the unfailing, unchangeable love of God had burdened me with needless condemnation and guilt. Just as I could never earn my salvation, I can never earn God's love.

"But I am poor and needy; yet the Lord thinketh upon me: Thou art my help and my deliverer ... " (Psalm 40:17, KJV).

At the time, I could write a list of reasons why I felt needy, but my thoughts were drawn instead to the word "yet." The psalmist was being honest about his feelings, but he didn't stop there.

The primitive root for the word "thinketh" is to twist or intertwine—literally to weave.[2] It means to think about, regard, or study like a skillful workman in the process of creativity. When the Lord thinks about us, it isn't linear, it's with the creative eye of a skillful weaver, an artist, discerning what the next color should be in his creation. He intertwines

---

2) "Hebrew Dictionary (Lexicon-Concordance) Keyword Studies (Translations-Definitions-Meanings), No. H2803," *Strong's (Hebrew and Chaldee Dictionary of the Old Testament)*. Accessed at: http://www.lexiconcordance.com/hebrew/2803.html.

His life, personality, and promises into everything He creates, then puts it deep into our hearts.

In Psalm 40, David was struggling against fierce enemies, isolation, and discouragement. But he gives us a window into victorious living as he looks in the face of the darkness around him, and with a heart determined to go after God, declares "yet." No matter how many battles life brings, God never changes. His love never fails. He is the Good Shepherd. I suspect this place of turning was an inspiration for many of David's songs.

The word "yet" means up until the present, from now into the future, still, even though, nevertheless, or, in spite of that.[3] Dark times cannot quench the "yet" of God. Nothing can separate us from Him, not even anger. Even though I may feel poor and needy, my God is looking at me with the eyes of a master craftsman who knows the perfect plan for my life. I can trust Him because I am His workmanship, His unique masterpiece, created in Christ Jesus. (Ephesians 2:10)

I was learning to live in the "yet" of God. He was teaching me how to answer the concerns of my heart when times were tough.

Our trials are real, never to be denied or glossed over, never to be diminished with verses void of compassion and mercy. But as we acknowledge the magnitude of our trials, we must remember there is another step to take. We must acknowledge the even greater reality that God is with us in the center of our circumstances. He is the "yet" that shines in the whirlwind, the "yet" that comforts our weary souls.

---

3) *Oxford North American English Dictionary.* S.v. "Yet." New York: Oxford University Press, 2017. Accessed at: https://en.oxforddictionaries.com/definition/us/yet.

CHAPTER TWENTY-ONE

Are You Ready?

My husband had a quirky kind of shyness. He rarely looked me in the eyes when we were close, never more than a quick glance. But after his near-death experience, he would stare into my eyes. At first it was a bit disarming, but at the same time, it fulfilled something deep inside that I didn't know I was missing.

"You have the most amazing blue to your eyes," he'd say.

Bill's eyes seemed different to me, too. They were clearer, bluer, and at times they seemed like they were filled with liquid love.

There were other changes, also. The irritability caused by steroids disappeared, and he had a peace that was contagious. There was a greater patience, a sweeter tone with his mom, and he loved looking into my eyes.

I could feel layers melting between us. It was as if we were falling in love all over again. Caring for him became sweeter, more like a privilege. I kissed his forehead, making sure not to crowd him. "Honey, do you ever miss the blue you saw in Heaven?"

Without hesitation he replied, "More than you know."

112

I wondered if Heaven was on his mind when he sat on the side porch enjoying the warm summer sun. He spent as much time out there as he could. We'd stretch the oxygen cord as far as it could reach and he'd sit in his chair for hours.

"This is my kind of weather," he'd say. "It's soft."

Bamma continued to hover with worry. No amount of reassurance satisfied her. I was thankful that she was there so I could get out of the house once in awhile. She and Bill seemed to enjoy each other's company and often talked for hours.

Bill was getting weaker, however. He could only walk a few feet now before his blood pressure would plummet. His love for God's Word had grown since his near-death experience. He said the Scriptures had more meaning to him now because all his doubt was gone.

When he wasn't on the porch, he mostly slept.

"He needs good food, Marjorie," Bernice instructed. I used to bristle and get defensive listing the healthy meals I was preparing, but Bill's appetite was diminishing. I understand now Bamma wasn't questioning my care; she was worried that he wasn't eating.

"I'm trying, but he only picks at what I bring him. He's just not hungry right now."

The sadness in our house grew stronger as if grief was making its approach. Bernice and I talked about Bill endlessly. "Maybe you should try giving him soup," or "Do you think he should go back to the hospital?" I had no answers. We reasoned together but neither one of us dared say what we knew in our hearts was happening.

One perfect day in early August, 2007, Bill's mom agreed to sit with Bill. He wasn't bed-bound, but he couldn't walk more than a few feet without the risk of falling. The neighbors had offered me the use of their pool while they were at work.

I floated around the pool, drinking in the peace. *Thank you, Lord, I so needed this.* Suddenly, a crystal clear question entered my mind.

Are you ready?

I immediately knew that the Lord was referring to becoming a widow. I hadn't thought about what Bill had shared in more than two years, but I knew exactly what the Lord was asking me.

I didn't answer. Instead, I thought about our long talks and prayers, and how much Bill had changed. I thought about the people he impacted with his story, and the special times he had with his mother. I considered how difficult life was getting for him, and how this vibrant, active man had been reduced to sleeping or sitting next to an oxygen machine 24 hours a day. Pictures of him crumpling to the floor from plummeting blood pressure haunted me, and the endless nausea and exhaustion still plagued him.

I knew God's plan didn't hinge on my answer, but instead I had the sense He was inviting my response for my own benefit. Amos 3:3 came to mind. *"Can two people walk together without agreeing on the direction?* (NLT). There's no stronger force than two in agreement. This is not a harsh demand, but an invitation to walk with intimacy of heart and mind. When there is common ground, moving forward is much easier.

Looking up at the cloudless, azure sky, I considered how many times Bill mentioned missing "the blue" he'd seen in Heaven: "more than you know." He was looking forward to something he'd had a taste of, something known. He looked for that touch of blue everywhere—in my eyes, in his children's eyes—but it never compared.

"Yes, Lord, I'm ready," I whispered as tears streaked my face.

Two weeks later, I was making dinner when I heard Bill's frantic call.

"I can't get air! Call the ambulance—I think I have pneumonia."

Once again, the paramedics came, only this time, Bill went with them. They transported him to the emergency room as I followed in my car. Surprisingly, I had no fear, only an enveloping peace. I knew the Lord was with me.

Bill didn't have pneumonia. The sarcoidosis had suddenly flared.

"We really can't do much more for him," said the doctor. "We have to get Bill off the steroids, but I'm concerned if we do that, he won't have enough oxygen generated by the machine he has at home."

After talking with the social worker, we decided that Bill should receive home hospice care so he could get the help he needed.

"We'll reevaluate in a few months," the social worker said kindly. "If he's better, he can come off hospice."

To my surprise, the doctor sent Bill home the next day. The medical staff assured us a hospice nurse would visit that afternoon.

We drove most of the way home in silence.

"Remember, honey, they said they'll reevaluate when you are better. You just need a little extra help right now, and then you can come off hospice."

Bill didn't respond.

The nurse came that afternoon, just as they promised. Next, the medical supply truck backed up the driveway.

We'd already moved Bill's bed into the living room. My stomach knotted as I watched them wheel in five, 50-gallon barrels of liquid oxygen, a portable commode, and a walker.

"He'll need two drums at a time," they instructed. "Plus, you'll have two for a back-up, and another in case one of them malfunctions."

"This is only temporary," I tried to reassure Bill's mom, who was leaning into the wall for support. Her face was pallid and drawn. "It's

only so he can get the oxygen he needs right now ... until he gets better."
She looked into my eyes. I was too afraid to say what I was fearing—that
he would not get better, but I sensed she was thinking the same thing.

CHAPTER TWENTY-TWO

In the Pavilion

No one expected things to move so fast. Bamma and I were taking turns sitting with Bill when he was awake. She kept offering soup, but Bill had no appetite. He seemed to be doing a little better since they switched him to the liquid oxygen. His mind was clear and he was peaceful.

Bamma was sitting on the porch when the hospice nurse arrived for a regular visit two weeks later. She didn't like to be in the way, so after announcing the nurse's arrival, she quickly disappeared into her apartment.

Bill's nurse was a perky, self-assured woman about 50 years old, with a broad smile and a calming demeanor. I was always relieved when she came, and I greeted her with a flood of questions. This time, she wanted to examine Bill first.

When she finished, I followed her outside and she gave me further instructions for administering medication. It must have been the Lord's prompting because, for the first time, I asked her what I should expect when the time came.

"Will Bill have convulsions?" I asked.

"No, don't worry about that. In Bill's case, his breathing will begin to slow down and the time *between* breaths will lengthen ... until ... " she paused to study my face. "Until it stops."

Tears filled my eyes. The nurse put her hand gently on my shoulder. "It's very tough," she said. "Try to hold on."

I nodded, swallowing my tears. "I'll try."

We walked to her car, and I thanked her for coming. "I have to visit a patient close by, but I will be back to see Bill in an hour or two. Just keep giving him the medicine as I instructed."

Bernice opened her door as the nurse disappeared down the driveway. "What did she say?"

"Nothing new with his condition," I sighed. "The nurse just gave me new instructions for his medicine, that's all."

"Did you write it down? You'll forget. You have to get this right," Bamma insisted.

I didn't answer because I was lost in my thoughts. *Why were they increasing the morphine? Why did I ask the nurse about his last moments? What if I do something wrong? This is too much for me to handle, Lord. Give me Your strength.*

I knew the Lord was with me. I had a peace and composure that was way beyond anything natural. It was as if He was holding my heart in the palm of His hands, freeing me from the weight of my fears, so I could do what I had to do.

Kyle pulled in the driveway right after the nurse left. He came regularly, even though this was a busy work season. Moments later, Jonathan and his family arrived too. I was relieved to see them all, but it also made me nervous.

Then another young man who looked up to Bill as a second father knocked on the door. He'd left work to come and visit.

Next, my neighbor and her two kids came through the door.

Lord, this is so strange. What's going on?

All the people closest to Bill had arrived at the same time, a perfect, divinely orchestrated gathering. We all sat in the parlor telling stories, laughing and happy, while taking turns talking with Bill in the next room. He could hear our chatter in the background, and I'm sure it was the perfect prescription to fill him with joy.

After an hour or so, without understanding why, I felt led to invite those who wished to come into Bill's room.

"Everybody, I think we should all gather around the bed."

Jonathan squeezed my elbow, "What are you saying? Dad isn't going to … " His words trailed off as he followed everyone to the bedside.

The kids from next door spoke up spontaneously, telling Bill what he meant to them. Tears began to flow.

"I'll never forget when you showed me how to tie my necktie for my first communion," said Chad, now a teenager.

"We love you, Dad," Jonathan and Kyle said as tears streamed down their cheeks.

Bill was able to express his love and gratitude to every person there while I administered his medicine.

"Take care of your mom," he said to his boys.

Bernice reached her arm through the crowd and made the sign of the cross on Bill's forehead. *Oh dear,* I thought. *Her heart must be breaking that I didn't call a priest … She didn't ask for a priest. Bill never did … Lord, let her know You're here.*

All through that early morning before everyone came, one of the songs I'd written years ago, "In God's Pavilion," kept playing over and over in my mind. So I leaned over and sang it softly in Bill's ear. I found out later, both our sons had arrived humming the that same song too.

Moments later, Bill took his last breath.

The family quietly left the room so I could be alone with him. Molly was sitting on the floor beside the bed, her big, brown eyes peeking out beneath her shaggy fur. I picked her up and placed her on the bed next to Bill so she could say goodbye, too. She wagged her tail as she instinctively moved to smell his breath, just as she had done every day since he became ill. First, she sniffed on the left, then walked across the pillow above his head and sniffed on the right. That didn't satisfy her, so she returned to sniff on the left again. Finally, little Molly laid down and rested her head on his neck. She knew he was gone.

"In God's Pavilion"

There shall no evil befall me
for in God's pavilion I stand.
He'll place my feet upon a rock
and hold me by the hand.
The Lord God, is my Shepherd,
He'll lead to pasture green.
From mountain tops to valleys,
upon His Word I'll lean.

Chorus:
In times of trouble I will hide
in the pavilion at His side
I'll trust in Jesus from the start
and His peace shall fill my heart.

© 1980 MARJI STEVENS

CHAPTER TWENTY-THREE

Is This How "Ready" Feels?

"For I am the LORD your God who takes hold of your right hand and says to you, Do not fear; I will help you." (Isaiah 41:13, NIV)

Kyle and Jon removed Bill's bed and hospital equipment from the living room the next day. The medical supply company came to pick up the drums of liquid oxygen. All the tubes and medicines were gone, every trace of hospice care removed. A few dust-covered paper corners torn from bandage wrappers littered the old pine floor where his bed had been. I stood frozen in the doorway staring at the empty space.

You asked me if I was ready, Lord. Is this how 'ready' feels?

There was a different kind of sadness in the house now. It was the sadness of something wonderful coming to an end. I questioned for a moment how saying yes had helped me. I believed it was the Lord, and I answered from my heart, so why did I feel so totally ill-equipped? I wondered if it had been the kind of question a surgeon asks a patient before major surgery. "Are you ready, Mrs. Stevens?" You comply, having no idea how difficult the recovery will be.

I like to think I'm always ready to say yes to God's will, but suddenly I realized my "yes" was permission to amputate one-half of me. The leg I'd depended upon to keep me balanced had been cut off. How would I walk now? How would I ever run with confidence again? How would I steady myself with half of me gone? How would I deal with the phantom pain that tried to convince me he was still here? How would I turn off the automatic responses of my heart only to turn and face the horror that I was talking to myself?

Fear rose in my heart. *What if I never recover? What if I can't do this?*

I do not doubt the Lord was trying to communicate that He was with me, but I could not hear, or sense, or feel. I was numb.

I felt guilty because a big part of me was relieved that it was over, happy to say goodbye to those dreaded symbols of sickness and struggle. I hated looking at them. I didn't want to hear the continuous drone of the oxygen machine. I was bone-tired from worry and medical decisions, and doctors and so much sadness.

One fear I'd never voiced was how death would come. I'd never witnessed someone's passing. I didn't know what to expect and it had frightened me. But his passing was peaceful. Now it was all behind us. We had watched his countenance change like the lifting of a delicate, rosy veil, carried into the presence of Jesus, beyond the "touch of blue," to be eternally enveloped with the full spectrum of Heaven's reward. I *knew* Bill was happy.

A sudden urge swept over me to open all the windows. I wanted to see the curtains billowing in a gust of fresh air to cleanse away every molecule of sickness and struggle. I wanted to wash the windows as if sadness had left a clammy film on every pane, obscuring the light. I wanted freshness, my own touch of blue. I wanted a new beginning, to step free from so many years of grappling with disease. We'd believed for a miracle while treating his symptoms. God chose this way. Bill had a brand new body now.

I tried to put the living room back in place, as if reorganizing that room would help me find normal again. I dared not feel. I couldn't think. Physical surroundings seemed like the only thing I had any control over.

My son Kyle responded to the sound of the couch being dragged across the living room floor and came to see what I was doing.

"Mom, do you really need to do that now?"

"I just want to get the living room back to normal."

Kyle stood watching me as I tossed the pillows on the floor and started jerking the couch closer to the window.

"I haven't washed these curtains in a year, and I want to get to the windows."

"Mom, stop," he said softly. "Come sit down. There will be plenty of time for windows, Mom. Rest. You're still in shock."

"But, I need to do this! You don't understand ... "

He took me by the shoulders and guided me to the kitchen table. "Sit, we have a lot to talk about."

Kyle and Jonathan took the reins planning the funeral. I went along with whatever they decided. We worked together to get the living room back together, and even washed the windows in time for the reception at our home. Even though I was numb, I felt a cushion of God's peace in my spirit. When I started to look beyond the moment, fear would well up inside. Each time this happened, the Holy Spirit would remind me: "Do not fear, for I am with you ... " (Isaiah 41:10, NASB).

Guests filed into the funeral home, filling the rows behind me. The guest book listed an amazing number attending. Dozens of Bill's former high school students came to pay their respects. It was so crowded that most of the people were unable to get inside. All this was happening around me like I was watching a movie, someone else's funeral. I vaguely remember someone helping Bamma to her seat, but I don't know how she got there or who took her back home.

This is happening to someone else. This isn't me. This isn't us.

I don't remember much about the day of the funeral, but one thing stands out very clear. It was a perfect, cloudless August day, with the deepest azure sky I'd ever seen. I thought of the "touch of blue" and how Bill must be rejoicing to be viewing it again—only this time with Jesus. "We don't have words in the English language to describe what I saw," he used to say.

The glimpse of Heaven made all the difference to Bill. It vanquished all his fear of dying and set a kind of seal upon his faith. Doubt was gone. The chain he'd struggled with was broken. The life on earth had lost its luster, and he forever longed to see that touch of blue again.

I had to hold on to the hope that the Lord would now bring Heaven's touch to me as well, enabling me to find my way through the colorless world before me, and somehow learn to live again.

CHAPTER TWENTY-FOUR

When the Casseroles Stop

After the funeral, my son Jonathan and his family came to spend the week, even though they only lived ten miles away.

"We thought you might like some happy grandbaby noises in the morning," my daughter-in-law said.

They were right. I loved having them there though I mostly sat and watched what was happening around me. With the added family there, I was very grateful for the extra food brought by my church.

When the doorbell rang, a woman I recognized from church stood smiling at me through the screen door.

"It was my turn to bring dinner," she said. "I hope you like what I've made—it's lasagna. We're all so sorry for your loss." She held out a huge roaster pan. "Please let us know if there's *anything* we can do. Julia will be bringing dinner tomorrow."

She couldn't stay. I thanked her and watched as she walked to her car. An incomprehensible hollowness knotted in my stomach as her car disappeared down the road. My throat tightened with tears. Part of me wished she'd stayed, and part of me was glad she hadn't. I closed the door and put the lasagna in the freezer. *That makes four lasagnas and one chicken-noodle dish.* While I had no desire to eat, I was grateful, and it was helpful to have the extra food while my son's family was there.

After a couple days however, the little ones weren't sleeping well. Jonathan and Autumn decided to return home early so the kids could be in their own beds.

Now it was just me, Bernice, and Molly, with an incomprehensible hole in the middle of our world.

Clumps of balled-up tissues dotted the living room. One part of me wanted to strip away the curtains and let the late afternoon sun flood into the room. Another part of me wanted to close the shades and hide in the dark. I didn't know what I wanted. It was difficult for me to make the smallest decision. I had the urge to clean out every drawer, rearrange the furniture, and scrub everything as hard as I could as if cleaning would somehow remove the sadness, but I had no energy. Yet another part of me wanted to curl up, pull the covers of misery over my head and let the world around me disappear.

For a few more days, people came with meals. Everyone was very sweet. "If there's anything we can do—*anything*—just call."

Then the casseroles stopped.

The cards dwindled. The phone stopped ringing. The kids got busy, and life moved on for everyone—everyone but me. I realized I was looking at the face of a steep, fractured mountain before me. There was no way to avoid the precipitous climb, the jagged cliffs and treacherous turns. I could only see a few steps ahead before the path curved and disappeared into the unknown.

In the beginning, people are attentive. Everyone wants to give their condolences. Often, this is at a time when the one suffering grief is so numb they hardly remember any of it.

Everyone processes this early phase differently. Some love the attention. Some don't want any. Some want to hide. Some don't want to be alone for one minute. What makes ministry to a widow or widower difficult is there is no set protocol to follow. That's why the Lord calls it a ministry. It's not done in our own strength. We have to follow the leading of the Holy Spirit who knows the perfect comfort for every broken heart.

People's reactions toward the one grieving also vary widely. Some believe the loving thing to do is leave you alone, out of respect for your privacy. Some are silent because they don't know what to say, or they're afraid to say the wrong thing, or worry they'll upset you. It's socially awkward, so many people just avoid it.

I remember trying to contact one friend, only to hear her voicemail greeting each time I called. My messages went unanswered, so a tough reality became clear: No one could do for me what I had to learn to do for myself.

My friends could show compassion, or be there when I was in trouble, but the day-to-day walk through grief was mine alone. I had to face the void in my empty house. I had to manage the challenge of long, lonely weekends. I had to learn to encourage myself in the Lord. I had to seek the Lord when anxiety gripped me and there was no one to talk to.

The church makes itself most visible in the first few weeks after the death of a spouse. But the greatest challenge comes long after the initial loss. We expect our widows to move on far more quickly than is realistic. Often the second and third years are the most difficult.

All the early attention is appreciated, but for the one who is grieving, the hard work comes long after the casseroles stop, when you're no longer on the front page of people's minds.

This was a tough truth to swallow. I became deeply offended with those I expected to be there—but weren't.

Lord, where are all my friends?

God helped me see I was entering another great challenge: the challenge to forgive.

CHAPTER TWENTY-FIVE

Beware of the Way of Offense

A person said to me one day, "I pass your house all the time and want to stop, but I decided I shouldn't do that until God is number one in your life."

I was furious—and hurt. She was judging my relationship with God. I knew that God would take the role of my husband, but I wasn't there yet. I wasn't used to living life on my own. In the meantime, I needed the encouragement and compassion of my friends.

Our journey is never a solitary one. The center of the Cross is vertical—representing the relationship between God and man, but the arms of the Cross are horizontal—representing the embrace of brothers and sisters in Christ. No one grows alone. We need a relationship with God, and the fellowship of His Body.

I wasn't sure if this was just my experience or if other widows had similar feelings. I decided to interview a few widows, and out of the 20 women I talked with, they all agreed that beyond a week of meals, the church was mainly silent.

forgiveness

What is this, Lord? There's a hole in the church. Without hesitation He replied, "I want you to help fill that hole."

I thought He would launch me into some sort of ministry to widows, but He let me know I had to heal first. The anger I still had in my heart had to give way to understanding.

I hated the feelings that accompanied the offense. For almost a year, I couldn't even drive on the grounds of the church without anger tightening my chest. God was gradually healing me, but I hadn't fully released it to Him. Choosing to forgive has to happen over and over until all the offense is gone.

Getting free of offense takes release and surrender to His will. It takes continued prayer and deliberate repentance for every negative thought, and every time I yielded to the temptation to talk about it. I knew the dangers of offense, because I'd taught on the subject in ministry years earlier. We're all susceptible to offense. The enemy knows exactly how to custom design the right situation to ensnare us.

Even when the offense is totally justified, it places us at a dangerous fork in the road. The word *offense* means to be morally outraged, but it also means *to be turned out of the way.*[4]

We have to make the deliberate choice to forgive. Offense can't be brushed off or treated lightly. We can't be nonchalant about it because taking no action becomes the wrong action. We have to choose to forgive, or find ourselves going the wrong way.

Forgiveness is more than a feeling. To forgive a wrong is not to condone the wrong. There are many situations when the act is almost unforgivable, but forgiveness frees us to move forward, and it frees the offender from our judgement. Only God is judge.

---

4) Benson, Joseph. "Commentary on Hebrews 12:12-14" *Commentary on the Old and New Testaments.* New York: T. Carlton & J. Porter, 1857. Accessed at: http://biblehub.com/commentaries/benson/hebrews/12.htm

The illustration that helps me understand forgiveness is this: picture a cage in your heart. When we don't forgive someone, that person remains locked in that cage, which means they are constantly with us. The act of forgiveness opens the cage in our hearts and lets them out. It's not a dismissal of their wrongdoing, but a release so God can deal with them, and we can move on and be healed.

Hebrews 12:13 says we are to make straight paths for our feet, lest we be turned out of the way. Natural paths are not straight. They meander and wind, like the path of a deer through the woods. If you are walking through the fields and see a straight path, it shows someone has applied effort to make it that way.

In a similar way, when we've been wounded by someone, we must be wary not to let offense turn us out of the way of healing. When we replay a hurt over and over in our minds, keeping it alive by constantly talking about it, we are traveling a dangerous course.

Matthew 24:10 speaks about the offense coming in the end times, "And then many will be offended, and shall betray one another, and shall hate one another" (KJV). It goes beyond our hurt feelings to what the devil is doing these days. Look around you, offense is everywhere. We have to rise above the norm through the strength of the Lord, and not give in to offense. We must be people of forgiveness.

When we refuse to forgive, harboring hurt in our hearts, we invite deception. The word "betray" in Matthew 24 means *to be handed over to an enemy.*[5] I place myself in an open, unguarded position when I allow offense to lead me this far. That's one reason why the Scripture admonishes us: "Do not let the sun go down while you are still angry,

---

5) "3860. Paradidómi," *HELPS™ Word-studies by Helps Ministries, Inc.* Accessed at: http://biblehub.com/greek/4236.htm

131

and do not give the devil a foothold," (Ephesians 4:26-27, NIV).

The next step in the way of offense is to "hate one another." 1 John 4:20 says, "Whoever claims to love God yet hates a brother or sister is a liar," (NIV).

When we entertain offense, we stand on the edge of the land of lies. Whether we become the liar, or open ourselves to believing the lies of the enemy, we're on shaky ground. "For whoever does not love their brother and sister, whom they have seen, cannot love God, whom they have not seen," (1 John 4:20b, NIV).

I felt abandoned by those I thought were best friends. People I'd known for decades were silent. It took me a long while before I saw the bitterness growing in my heart, because I felt my offense was justified. It took me years before it was finally cleared away. Unforgiveness is toxic to our health—physical, emotional, and spiritual. To me, it was a poison that went so deep that just when I thought I'd finally forgiven those people, it would reappear. I knew I wasn't healed when fresh anger would rise every time the subject of church came up.

Bamma could see that I was holding onto hurts because it came out in our conversations. She'd say, "Marjorie, you have to let it go." I was going down the road of self-pity. She kept saying, "If you don't let it go, it's going to make you sick."

Our progression through grief is greatly influenced by forgiveness. I had to forgive the doctors who I believed had dropped the ball. I had to forgive friends for things they did or didn't do while I was at my lowest moments as a widow.

God showed me that forgiveness was life and breath for me. Only through forgiveness could He renew my resilience and love, so I could walk into the future. He showed me that every time I felt offense rise in my heart I had to choose to forgive, even if I didn't have feelings of forgiveness. I learned forgiveness is not dismissing a wrong, it's releasing myself from a deadly poison and opens the door for my healing, and theirs. Jesus gave us the example to follow when He hung on the Cross of Calvary and said: *"Forgive them, Father,* for they know not what they do," (Luke 23:34, KJV). Jesus told Peter he had to forgive a brother who sins against him *"seventy-seven times,"* (Matthew 18:22, NIV).

I was convicted of my own insensitivity towards grieving friends, even my own mother when she was first a widow. I was impatient for her to move on. Her neediness was irritating. Now I could understand what my mother was going through. I grieved bitterly over the love I could have shown her. *Lord, please tell my mother how sorry I am. I didn't understand, Lord, forgive me.*

Seeing my own need for forgiveness was a huge step toward helping me forgive others. As painful as it was, the results were wonderful. I knew when I was finally healed, because I no longer had that tug in my gut when certain subjects came up. My heart was finally clear.

The truth is, I was never abandoned by the ones God had chosen to walk closely with me. Both my sons were present and tender. My daughter-in-law Autumn called me *every* day for more than a year. My friend Coleen patiently listened to my woes over and over, even letting me call in the middle of the night when the need arose. Another friend, Jeannie, kept me laughing and took me to the movies. These individuals were like angels appointed and sent to hold up my arms. They encouraged, listened, passed the tissues, took me places, restored me to joy, and reminded me of the Truth.

When I was finally free of unforgiveness, I could see the blessings I had. We'll always have people in our lives who just don't get it. We have to put them in God's hands, guard our hearts from picking up offense, and be grateful for the ones who do understand.

CHAPTER TWENTY-SIX

The New Porch Swing

I've always had a designated quiet time spot, somewhere set aside for me to meet with the Lord. The habit started when I was a brand-new Christian. If I found the time to sit, with two small boys, I didn't want to have to hunt for my Bible, or find Cheerios in my journal, or discover my pen had been confiscated. I didn't want my Bible buried under newspapers or kicked under the couch. I wanted it waiting for me.

My first quiet time place was an over-stuffed chair I'd found for $7 at a garage sale. I reupholstered it with a remnant of floral fabric and a staple gun. That chair lasted me for a while, but was eventually adopted by the boys for Saturday morning cartoons and pancakes. I couldn't handle the syrup on my Bible, so I went in search of a new place.

The old, abandoned camper parked in the fields behind our house proved to be the perfect place. It was filled with wasps so nobody would ever bother me there. I had to get used to the wasps floating lazily past my head, and walking across my books, but I never once got stung. I was so determined to get alone with God, I didn't care what was keeping me company.

Then there was the closet. I read in Matthew 6:6, "When you pray, go into your closet, shut the door, and pray to your Father in secret." So I did ... only it was Bill's closet. I was buried in the back of his closet one day and didn't hear him come home. When he opened the closet door, I squealed, "Hi!" After Bill peeled himself down from the ceiling, he made it clear to me that his closet was off-limits from then on.

Then there was the time I decided to climb into Bill's deer stand behind our house. Unfortunately, the wind blew so hard that day, it sent the ladder tumbling down. I had no choice but to wait to be missed—I was 10 feet in the air. Bill eventually came looking for me and put the ladder back in place. All I heard as he walked down the hill was, "Good grief, I've married Lucille Ball."

My location for quiet time seemed to change for each new season of growth. It's no wonder God gave me a new place to meet with Him when I became a widow.

I just knew the minute I saw the swing in Home Depot it was meant for me. For 40 years of marriage, I'd kept my wiggle under the strictest control because I was married to a man who hated to move the slightest bit when he sat. He was forever telling me to "SIT STILL!" If we were going to sit next to each other I couldn't wiggle, jiggle, twitch, or shuffle if I wanted it to last. I even had to master the art of itching in slow motion. We tried a glider once, but I'd be on my end trying to get a good glide going and he'd be on his end braking. So after one too many frustrated "discussions," we decided to give the glider away.

I showed the Home Depot clerk which swing I wanted, but when he wheeled out the huge carton full of pieces, my heart sank. It never occurred to me I would have to assemble it—that was always Bill's job.

Little did I know I was running up against a common problem for widows: the awkward challenge of asking for help. Nobody likes being a bother, and I can't think of anything more bothersome than assembling something.

There was no way I was going to ask either of my sons for help without first trying it myself, because they were so busy with work and families.

"I can do this." I told myself. "Your word says I can do all things when You strengthen me. Right, Lord?"

The box was too heavy to lift, so when I got it home, I had to drag it from the car. Bernice stuck her head out the door.

"Marjorie, what did you buy now?"

"What do you mean NOW?" I replied, out of breath. She changed the subject. "You can't put that thing together yourself, you'll get hurt."

"It's a swing, and I'm going to try. I don't want to bother the boys— they're busy enough."

"Suit yourself," she said, but before she closed the door I heard her tell the dog, "Molly, your mother is going to kill herself one of these days. She just won't listen."

"Good night, nurse," I mumbled, continuing to drag the box across the driveway.

To my surprise, it wasn't as difficult to put together as I thought it would be. It was just awkward because of its size. I finished in less than an hour and was positioning it on the patio when the door opened again.

"You can't put that there! You'll have to move it."

"What?"

"I can't see when the neighbors pull into their driveway. It blocks my view. You can't encase me in here completely, you know. I'll go nuts."

I didn't bother addressing that comment. I dutifully yanked it to the other side of the patio so she could continue spying on the neighbors.

The next morning, when my alarm went off at 5:30 a.m., I got my coffee, Bible and journal and went to the swing to watch the sunrise. However, I was rudely alerted that the cushions were soaked with rain. Moving cushions in and out every day was not for me, so I decided to move the swing from the patio to the side porch. That way it would stay dry under the roof.

Since the awning on my swing was no longer necessary, I unscrewed the bolts to remove it. Just then, a sudden gust of wind whipped one end out of my hand. It did a 180-degree spin and cracked me square in the mouth. As my lip swelled to bulbous proportions, I dragged the swing up two patio steps and attempted to turn the corner at the end of the porch. Instead I got the swing lodged between the porch railing and Bamma's front door. That's when I heard her door squeak open again.

"Marjorie! You're not going to leave it *there* are you? No one will be able to get in my door! What if there's a fire?"

I just glared at her.

She silently observed my swollen lip and closed the door. I was spared having to hear what she said to the dog.

Finally, I swallowed my pride and called my neighbor.

"Can you come hel-b me?" I stammered with my fat lip.

"What's wrong with your mouth?"

"It's a long story."

"You sound like you've been to the dentist and got a big, fat shot of novocaine," she laughed. "Let me finish up what I'm doing here and I'll pop over."

For the next hour I iced my lip and avoided my mother-in-law. I was also discovering that beyond the embarrassment of asking for help, you have to wait for the time when it's convenient for others to come to your rescue. Waiting has never been my forté.

It had only been six months since Bill passed, so I was pretty emotional about the littlest discoveries. My mind jumped from one anxious thought to another: *What will I do about cleaning the gutters? What if the car battery needs charging? What if the toilet overflows?* Soon, I was in tears.

As my neighbor came around the corner of her property, she spotted my swing. "Why do you want to move that big thing on the porch?" she called out as she crossed the lawn. "Is it gonna fit?"

"Hi ... wet cushions ... don't know, I neb-er measured."

She looked at my lip and rolled her eyes. "Oh, geez, why didn't you call me sooner? Look at you."

We both started laughing at this point. "Come on, let's do this," she said.

With her help, it only took a few minutes to get the ginormous swing frame onto the side porch.

"It fits!" I squealed.

"Lucky for you," she said sarcastically. We settled onto the swing. "This is comfy," she said, patting the cushions. Her eyes twinkled, "You've been crying again. Your eyes are as puffy as your fat lip."

"I'm worried about how I'm going to do all the stub-ff around here myself. I can't afford to hire someone to do eb-erything. My sons are so busy already. What ib-ff the lights go out in the middle of the night and I hab-b to find my way down in that awful basement? How am-b I going to get the air conditioner in the window?"

"But it's September," she said. "Why are you worried about the air conditioner?"

"And what about the seb-tic tank?"

"Whoa, you're making me tired. I know it's very overwhelming right now, but one day at a time," she said, standing up. "Look, I know it's easy for me to say that, but that's all you can do. We love you. People will be more than happy to help you, I'm sure." She gave the cushions one last tug. "Looks great. Here, give me a hug. Sorry, I can't stay—I'm cooking something. Call me if you need any more help." I got up and gave her a big hug.

"Thanks so much," I said. "I owe you."

"You sure do," she called over her shoulder.

I was so grateful for such a good friend and neighbor. She always lifted my spirits with her wonderful sarcastic humor. But as I watched her disappear around the corner of her house, I became painfully aware that I was the only one sitting on the swing.

CHAPTER TWENTY-SEVEN

Surrender and Acceptance

Sifting through Bill's desk, I found page after page of his life. Calendars. Journals. Scraps of paper with his handwriting, an amalgam of thoughts and activities, each requiring a fresh goodbye.

I took a break from the intensity to sit on my swing. The vapor rising from my coffee mug swirled in the crisp chill of the morning, steaming my glasses. I closed the top button on my sweater, pulled the quilt over my knees, and opened my Bible. "Anxiety in the heart of man weighs him down … " (Proverbs 12:25a, NASB).

Help me, Lord. I don't want to be weighed down, but everything seems to be overwhelming me.

Sorting through Bill's desk was only the beginning. I had bureaus and closets, his hunting gear, and then there was the basement. I couldn't toss things out like I usually would because they represented pieces of our life together. Part of me wanted to throw out everything that might remind me of him, but equally as strong was the desire to hold on to it all.

Do I keep this or throw it out? Donate it? Have a garage sale? Save it for the grandkids? If I get rid of this, will I regret it later?

Then there were the personal things like toiletries, his razor, his comb. Everything came with a memory connected to it and required a decision. It was overwhelming.

There's an internal "clutter" that also comes with loss. There are so many details to remember, and so many new things to learn. Confusion. Exhaustion. Difficulty focusing. Trouble remembering facts. I also found I had little patience for confusion and noise, and could only handle small doses of my happy and very energetic grandchildren. I was not myself ... no matter how hard I tried to be.

I've discovered how important it is to pay attention to my internal climate. Talking things through helps enormously. It's important not to deny feelings or let them shape your world.

My swing is the place I go to "unclutter" my heart. I've tried being brave. I've tried being an overcomer, but the way through this valley isn't paved with determination. It's paved by surrender and acceptance of the comfort He so lavishly pours out on those who mourn. In Philippians 4:6-7, we're encouraged to cast our anxieties and burdens on the Lord, and in exchange, He promises to give us peace that surpasses our understanding and that will be a guard over our heart and mind.

But when crisis strikes, God doesn't withhold His peace until we can lay our burdens down. I know He carries us. His love transcends any spiritual practice on our part. Before we could pray, or believe, or read Scripture, He loved us enough to die for us. In the beginning, I was too shaken to sit and do much else but cry. Yet the Lord didn't wait for me to ask before He comforted me.

Taking care of the emotional clutter is so important. An anxious heart weighs us down. It's like dragging bags of groceries around all day because we don't know well enough to put them in the cupboards. Those habits of holding on to hurts die hard. In my family, we were taught to get your mind off the problem and it would go away.

At that time, I enjoyed watching a TV program called *Hoarders*. It's a show about people who accumulate so many things—sometimes even garbage—in their homes, the possessions collect until there are only narrow pathways left from room to room. They become blind to the conditions they have created, accepting it as normal. Many of the people interviewed had suffered major losses in their lives, and at the start of the show, a voiceover states that hoarding can be a mental illness.

I was journaling one day when another illustration suddenly fluttered across my mind. It was a drawing of a person's torso which had a large window right in the center so you could look in. Inside was an ugly pile of garbage with flies buzzing all around. Next to the pile stood Jesus, shrugging His shoulders in bewilderment. The caption read: Don't, hoard your hurts.

I quickly grabbed paper and pencil and drew the cartoon image I'd seen. I knew the person was me. All the hurts I'd been trying to get off my mind were actually putrefying in my heart.

Resentment lay like thick grease at the bottom of the pile—resentment about having to be a caregiver again. First it was my mother, then my husband, then my mother-in-law. I also saw offenses piled up from thoughtless comments by people who didn't understand loss, didn't know what to do or say, so they stayed away. And on top of everything was anger, swarming like flies.

I wept as He opened my eyes to see what I'd become accustomed to carrying. "This is not how I want you to live," He said.

Lord, I don't want my heart to look like this.

142

Now I understood the bewilderment on the face of Jesus in my picture. He'd already paid the price to have every inch of garbage carried far away. He bore the pain of every hurt, every offense, every bitter emotion. They all belonged to Him now—He bought them on Calvary. Not only were my sins nailed to the cross, so were my circumstances. He was well acquainted with every grief and loss I was experiencing and I could trust Him to bear those too.

I grabbed my notebook and started to write down everything I saw from the pile. I scribbled out everything I was angry about, every offense, every disappointment. Page after page, I poured out my heart. In Matthew 10:14, Jesus instructed the disciples to "shake the dust off their feet" if they weren't received well or their instruction heeded. It's a good practice to get into the habit of doing each night. Before you go to sleep, shake off all the negatives so you don't drag the dirt of today onto the carpet of tomorrow. Jesus waits for us to empty our hands of yesterday's burdens, so He can replace them with the blessings of today.

The path through loss is paved with surrender and acceptance. Moving on does not mean we walk a straight line, checking off the steps like lists we make. It's a walk intimately mapped out by Jesus. Sometimes we go forward, sometimes we circle back. But ultimately, we come through it. No matter how we climb or descend on our journey, every step is precious to the Shepherd of our souls.

I put my notebook down and drained the last drop of coffee in my mug. The sun had crested the pine trees and felt hot upon my lap. I laid my head back against the cushion of my swing, closed my eyes, and soaked in His merciful peace.

CHAPTER TWENTY-EIGHT

Time Reset

My internal clock was reset the day Bill died.

I'll never look at the fourteenth of the month in the same way. It was the day my world changed, the day I went from wife to widow, from confident foresight to groping in the dark. I went from knowing who I was, what I liked, and where I was going, to needing an entirely new identity and road map for the future.

At first I counted the hours—then, the days. Bernice and I often started our morning conversations with: "Can you believe it's been __ number of days already?" Then it went to weeks and months. Even years later, the date found its way into our conversation.

"Can you believe it's been ___ years already?"

The journey through loss is not just resetting your internal clock, it's resetting your life.

I was suddenly thrust into a whole new world, one without Bill. I had to learn how to walk by myself, how to think independently, how to battle the emotional bullies, and learn how to lean on God alone.

Because I met Bill when I was 17, much of my maturity and identity as a woman was shaped with him beside me. I ran my own business, and traveled in ministry while Bill continually encouraged me to keep spreading my wings. My dependence on Bill was not because I was a weak woman; it was because I was deeply in love.

For the first two years, no one had to tell me when the fourteenth of each month was close. I knew it instinctively. An internal calendar kept record of how many weeks and months it had been. As the date approached, there was an increase in anxiety and sadness. Often I had more aches and pains. Mostly, I'd just lose my motivation to do anything. I can't explain how many times I laid on the couch wondering what was wrong with me only to realize: *Oh, it's the fourteenth again.*

At the time, I didn't know this was a normal part of grief. I'd read Elizabeth Kübler-Ross's classic book on the five stages of grief: denial, anger, bargaining, depression, and acceptance. To me, there was a whole lot missing from that list, including physical pain, anxiety, and this strange internal clock reset.

I also discovered that the stages of grief are not like grade levels we graduate from at particular times. When it comes to grief, I'm not a fan of lists and stages because few fit the mold. Grief is so dependent on the kind of relationship the individual had, the length of time invested in the relationship, one's age, personality, experiences, and available support, to name just a few. For example, a relationship where one suffered abuse will bring a different kind of grief, maybe even relief, versus that of an elderly couple who have walked arm-in-arm for 50 or 60 years. This is why we can't reduce the significance of grief by labeling it with stages.

Sometimes I moved through an entire stage in one day. It felt like one mini-funeral after another, as I faced each memory and learned to let go.

I had to be careful not to compare myself to what other widows did, or to what I read in books on grief.

I met a dear sister in the Lord while working at my part-time job at the craft and antique co-op. She understood grief. Her 16-year-old son had died suddenly nine years earlier.

"I can tell when the fourteenth is coming. Is that normal?" I asked.

"Definitely," she said. "Even to this day, I get sad on the date of his death."

"What do you do?"

"In the beginning, I just cried and slept. I prayed. Often, my husband's reaction was different. We tried not to let our personal grief create expectations for each other. He dealt with our son's death differently than I did. We had to accept the fact that it's a personal journey even for couples."

She thought a minute. "Later on, I tried to plan an activity on, or near, that date, giving me something to look forward to. If my husband was at work, or wanting his own time, I'd go to a light-hearted movie with a friend, or go out to lunch. I didn't always want to talk about it. I just didn't want to be alone."

"That's reassuring," I sighed.

"And don't be surprised if you ache from head to toe on those days. Grief can cause physical pain, too."

"Really? I'm so glad you told me this. My fibromyalgia has been really bad lately."

"I'm willing to bet your pain load will decrease significantly as you're further along in healing," she smiled.

Tears caught in my throat. Every time she reassured me that what I was experiencing was normal, I felt tremendous relief. I'd heard about people who never pulled out of grief, who couldn't move forward. I didn't want to be like that; I wanted to grieve with some measure of excellence. She was a vibrant woman, successful at her job, and sweet-spirited. With the Lord's help, she had managed to navigate through her terrible loss.

It's very helpful to have a friend who has walked in your shoes. I noticed I felt better inside every time we were together—even if we didn't talk about loss.

Gradually, just as she said, the months and years began to pass and the fourteenth blended in with all the other days. Even so, nearly a decade later, I'm still inclined to plan something fun around Bill's birthday, or our anniversary.

CHAPTER TWENTY-NINE

A New Dance

Grief can sneak up on you. There were strong, hopeful times, when I was sure things were better. Then, I'd swing back into deep sadness. My emotions were unpredictable. The first year was tough, but for me, the second and third years were much harder. The finality of Bill's death was sinking in, along with the stark reality that I really was on my own.

About a year after Bill's passing, I went to my son's 40th birthday party anticipating fun with family and friends, but I left before the cake was even served. As more couples arrived, I could feel myself begin to sink. *Bill should be here, Lord. This isn't right.*

No matter how I tried to enter into the festivities, I felt removed. Their conversation focused on summer plans and day trips. One couple had just retired and were planning a trip abroad. My throat tightened and I fought to hold back the tears as I considered the empty summer stretching out ahead of me. Now it seemed all I had to look forward to was watching TV with my 90-year old mother-in-law and the dog.

Determined to shake the bitter taste of grief, and the urge to get angry at their lack of sensitivity, I left the conversation and went inside to help the ladies in the kitchen. I tried entering into the chatter, but I had nothing to contribute.

I felt invisible.

All I wanted to talk about was how empty and lost I felt. *Do you know how much this hurts, people? Do you know how lucky you are to have the husbands you are criticizing? Does anyone care beyond shallow condolences?*

I was shocked by my anger. They had all said, "Sorry for your loss," (I grew to despise that line) then quickly moved on to talking about coupons and the latest happenings on Facebook. But what did I expect? Their world had not changed; they were in different seasons of life.

I had to learn to watch my words. Telling a random person about being a widow accomplishes nothing. It isn't good news. It's a reality no one wants to think about.

I discovered that most people, especially young wives, wanted to change the subject, and escape from any prolonged discussion of widowhood. Talking about losing a husband ignited too much fear in them.

"I'd die if anything happened to my husband," stuttered one young mother at the party.

It wasn't long before my smile disappeared, and their happy voices echoed in the distance as if I'd been moved to isolation in a room far away. I'd hoped that being with people would help overcome the sting of another family gathering without my husband, but it didn't happen. Grief managed to make its unsympathetic appearance. I felt like a drag on everyone's fun, so I opted to go home.

As I walked across the field to my car, a loathsome anxiety welled in my stomach. *Why such a hurry to get home? What for? He won't be there.* Still I longed for the safety of my house. *I'll sit on my porch swing.*

"Mom!" Jonathan came hurrying up to me. "You're going home already? Are you okay?"

"I can't do this, Jon. I'm sorry. I'm just struggling right now."

"I understand." He wrapped his arms around me. "I love you, Mom. Don't worry, you'll come through this."

I opened all the windows in the car and headed down the country roads, feeling invigorated by the cooler evening air. I took a slight detour, turning onto my favorite gravel road. It was lined by giant trees with arching branches that touched across the road. Shimmering sunlight pirouetted through the tree limbs, and the pale blue, July sky peeked shyly through the lush green canopy. My conversation with Bill came to mind again.

Honey, do you miss the blue?

More than you know.

I wanted to memorize the moment, drink in the beauty, allow it to leave its imprint upon my soul. I pulled over to the side of the road and turned off the engine.

Into my imagination streamed the vision from years ago, and I heard the tap-tap-tap of the conductor's wand. I wanted to glide across the dance floor with ease and grace, but my feet wouldn't move. Then I heard Him whisper: "Do you remember? Stay on the toes of your Father's shoes, and keep in the dance."

"Yes, Lord, I remember."

"Lean in, daughter. Lean in."

The light through the trees slowly faded into muted twilight. The memory of so much loss brought fresh tears. *Lord, I feel so broken. Help me to trust You.*

Trust is the shine on the shoes that would carry me across the dance floor into the future. Trust would keep me going forward.

How do you dance with God when your feet won't move? He will carry you. All He asks is that we believe, lean into Him, and reach for His embrace.

I drove the rest of the way home in peace. His comfort had come. New confidence had risen on the notes of His encouragement, and I knew I would not just make it through, I would make it through victoriously.

Later, I called my son, "Will you forgive me for leaving your birthday party and getting all emotional?"

"Mom," he replied softly, "We love you ... not to worry."

CHAPTER THIRTY

Practice Gratitude

Mountains of paperwork collected on my desk. I was still getting used to handling the household bills. It seemed more confusing than it should be and my stomach knotted every time I approached it. Sometimes I couldn't remember if I'd written a check or not. I didn't want to face the fact that this was now my job—one to be completed without Bill's help.

It was overwhelming to think that the entire house, and car, plus care for his mother, was on my shoulders. I felt suffocated by the responsibility. In the first year, the furnace and hot water tank went. Then Bill's car went on the fritz, and I was advised to get a new one. These were giant purchases; we had always made them together.

Kyle reassured me. "Mom, give it time. You don't have to do it all in one day."

"I feel like I'm losing my ability to think," I said.

"Mom, you'll be fine. Don't worry. Take it slow. We'll help you."
Both my sons told me that frequently. As a matter of fact, everyone told me that.

Lord, I don't know what "fine" feels like anymore. How do I get there? What if I can't?

I pushed my chair away from my desk, disgusted with how confused and worked up I was getting. Grabbing my favorite flannel shirt off the bench in the kitchen, I poured myself a cup of coffee, and retreated to the porch swing.

I hate the feeling of being overwhelmed, Lord. I hate that nothing feels normal. Will I ever find my way through this? Where do I start?

It was beginning to get nippy and the air was crisp and clean. I could feel the muscles in my shoulders begin to relax. The autumn leaves were just past peak, silhouetted against a cloudless October sky. I will never look at a blue sky the same way.

My stomach knotted. *Bill would have been deer hunting now. This is the kind of day he longed for.* That thought took me back to when I used to watch him prepare for the first hunt. It was a science. Everything was hung outside the night before so it smelled like fresh air. I had to wash everything with unscented detergent, and then he'd spray it with some foul-smelling concoction that was supposed to attract game. But the part I remember the most was his wide-brimmed camouflage hat that pushed his hair down and made it curl around his ears.

Tears grabbed at my throat. I ached for his arms around me. *Lord* ... The thought that I would never be close to him again was intolerable. I forced myself to turn my attention to the sound of the wind rustling the crispy leaves on the small tree next to the porch. The sun fell softly across the porch, touching my face like a warm kiss, and a curious thought entered my mind.

"I want you to practice gratitude."

Practice? I thought for a minute. I wasn't hearing the Lord say *"feel* grateful," or "you should be *more* grateful." Instead, it seemed He was giving me a loving invitation to walk through another door towards healing.

Practice is intentional. It requires discipline and focus, not necessarily inspiration. It is like learning an instrument. It means rehearsing something until it becomes second nature.

Loss of any kind can blind us. We can get so focused on what we've lost that it's easy to miss the blessings that still remain. A friend of mine lost a sister she was very close to. She said that she became so consumed with grief over losing her that she lost track of the two wonderful brothers she still had. Her grief seemed to be locking them out of her life, until one day her brother softly reminded her, "I'm still here." She suddenly realized the big, beautiful blessing standing in front of her. With a great swell of gratitude, she threw her arms around his neck and took a big step towards finding healing.

Practicing gratitude seemed very mechanical and insincere at first, but I started looking for *anything* in my surroundings to be grateful for. "Thank you for my swing. Thank you for crisp fall air. Thank you for a warm blanket over my knees." I was amazed how challenging it was at first.

"Lord, I am so grateful for Your love. I'm so grateful that You are here with me, that You'll never leave me or forsake me. I'm grateful that I will come through this time because You promise to turn my mourning into dancing."

I could see how gratitude changed the climate of my heart. As I stopped focusing on what was missing in my life I could see the good that was happening all around me. Though my gift of singing was gone, in its place was a passion for art as never before. I had new friends who were artists too. When we got together, we didn't focus on our problems—we got lost in the joy of creativity and friendship.

I was also beginning to get speaking invitations again. It was a joy to share about God's faithfulness to the brokenhearted.

I was experiencing wonderful success selling my things at the co-op. I had plenty to keep me busy creating more art to sell.

God wanted me to remember these things when I got down. On a beautiful fall day, it's easy to be grateful, but I understood He wanted me to *practice* gratitude so it would become second nature to look for His blessings. Many times over the next winter, I stood at the window watching the snow pile high, when grey days seem endless. Those were the empty days, when I was uninspired to create, when the silence was deafening, and my heart felt hollow. That's when His gentle reminder would come, "Tell me what you're grateful for."

"Thank you for the snow. Thank you how every flake is so unique. Thank you that in this silence I can hear Your voice more clearly. Thank you for my home so warm and comfortable."

Gratitude is a powerful tool, not just on the journey through grief, but on the journey of life. Listing what I was thankful for didn't eliminate the struggle, or deny the intensity of my feelings. It wasn't positive thinking, or an artificial bandaid to make me appear more victorious. It was an honest assessment of His endless lovingkindness. It focused my attention on the moment, on the blessings present ... even in the dark.

CHAPTER THIRTY-ONE

Precious in His Sight

Occasionally in upstate New York, we have a glorious February thaw. The air suddenly turns warm, and for a brief couple of days, you can enjoy a taste of spring. It soars into the 60s and everyone goes outside to enjoy the sunshine and the hope of winter ending.

I bundled up to take a walk, but soon my jacket was tied around my waist. The warmth of the sun felt glorious on my back. *Bill would have reveled in this.*

I thought about the healthy Bill, who loved to take long walks in the fields behind our house. He'd come home from work, change his clothes, and immediately go outside. "I need this," he would say.

Bill taught ninth grade. He was on his feet lecturing, answering questions and supervising hundreds of kids all day. When he came home, he didn't want to talk or problem-solve, he wanted *quiet*.

For years, he'd get me out of bed at 6 a.m. "Come on, get your gear on, we'll walk to the corner and get coffee." We even walked in the winter when it was dark in the morning. "Come on, it's good for us," he'd say.

I shuddered at the images of him failing. I wanted my walk in this brief February thaw to last forever. It was late afternoon and the sun was low in the sky. The trees edging the fields along the horizon took on a brilliant luminescence against the charcoal bank of clouds behind them. Even though the trees were stripped and bare, the sun's radiance on their branches made them appear as if they were dipped in gold.

I paused to contemplate how any artist would be able to capture such magnificence and have the painting look believable.

Lord, You are radiant in all Your glory. I can't imagine the unfathomable beauty of Heaven.

A gentle thought entered my mind, "Bill was radiant through his storm."

Now different pictures flooded my mind, not of sadness, but images of a man facing the end of his life with courage and dignity. Images of a praying man with his Bible open on his lap crystallized in my mind, images of a man at peace, even in the midst of his personal storm.

I can remember my mother telling me how she admired anyone who endured hardship without one word of complaint. She often boasted about her friend, " ... the thing I love about her is she *never* complains." Usually, she'd rehearse that story right after I finished complaining.

Ever since I became a Christian, I've prayed that the Lord would make me the kind of woman who is able to go through trials sweetly, without growing bitter, angry or demanding.

1 Peter 3:3-4 is a verse I often prayed.

"Do not let your beauty be that outward adorning of arranging the hair, of wearing gold, or of putting on fine apparel; but let it be the hidden person of the heart, with the incorruptible ornament of a gentle and quiet spirit, which is very precious in the sight of God," (NKJV).

157

I couldn't think of anything I wanted more than for the Lord to look at my heart and call it "precious." I knew it was the work only God could do, but I wanted to yield in every way possible. If there was anytime I needed Him working in my heart, it was now.

Fear was a big enemy. It came disguised in anxiety, depression, overeating, and not wanting to leave my home. Fear accompanied every new responsibility. I feared the responsibility of caring for my mother-in-law, Bernice. I feared losing my temper at her. Most of all, I feared the strength of my own emotions. I wanted the inner beauty of 1 Peter 3:4.

Peter shows us it's the *"hidden beauty of the heart"* that Jesus is after. Not the beauty that fades with time, but the life of Christ shining in our inner person, transforming us into His likeness.

To ornament means to arrange, and put in order, to embellish and decorate. (I guess that makes God our "interior decorator.") He removes the old, broken, sinful ways and fashions the beauty of Heaven in our hearts. He ornaments us with the fruits of His Spirit, which are "love, joy, peace, longsuffering, kindness, goodness, faithfulness, gentleness and self-control," (Galatians 5:22-23, KJV).

So, what are some of those precious qualities?

Gentleness is the Greek word *praotes* which is also defined as mildness or meekness. It is the ability to lay down your will for the will of another.[6] For the believer, *praotes* is the fruit (product) of the Holy Spirit; it is never something humanly accomplished.

Another quality the Lord calls precious is a quiet spirit.

In the Greek, *quiet* means "undisturbed and undisturbing." It is a tranquility arising from within. It's also characteristic of meekness.

Quiet is also a combination of two Greek words which mean "the ability to keep one's seat,[7] to hold one's possession or condition"

When I read that, a picture formed in my mind of a w
down holding on to the sides of her chair. People were try
off her seat, but she held on tight. The caption under the picture read,
"This is precious."

One of the hardest things to grasp as a Christian is the idea in
Ephesians 2:6 that we have been raised with Christ and are seated in
heavenly places in Christ Jesus. How is it that we're here, but we're
there at the same time? I can't explain it. This, however, was the image I
thought of when I read the definition of a quiet spirit. The devil wants to
knock us off our seat, and will conspire to use circumstances to convince
us we don't have a firm foundation.

However, when we remain seated in our faith no matter what is
happening, this is precious in the sight of God—more precious than
any other kind of beauty. When our emotions threaten to rocket us into
despair, but we remain seated in our beliefs, when we feel broken and
lonely, or paralyzed with anxiety and fear about the future, if we hold on,
in faith, to the truth of His Word—this is precious to the Father.[6]

Like the trees I saw on my walk, all radiant with the sun shining upon
them, our radiance through the storms of life will be because of the One
who hold us.

After dinner, I went out on my swing. Once again the thought came
to me: *You are radiant through this storm.* Now I understood it was God's
promise to carry me every step of the way. If my mind or emotions try
to contradict His truth, all I have to do is sink into the gift of His gentle
Spirit, hold tight to that seat of faith, and know that His light and life
alone will make me radiant through the storm.

6) "4236. Praotés," *HELPS™ Word-studies by Helps Ministries, Inc.* Accessed at: http://biblehub.com/greek/4236.htm.

7) "2272. Hedraios, Echo," *Strong's Exhaustive Concordance.* Accessed at: http://biblehub.com/greek/2272.htm.

CHAPTER THIRTY-TWO

Come, Let Us Magnify the Lord

It was a two-sweater morning, overcast and damp. I took my coffee outside anyway and settled on the swing, hoping to clear my mind. I was trying to remember to practice gratitude, and it was helping, but anxiety had become a tenacious companion. Every morning, waves of suffocating anxiety clenched my stomach, starting the day with dread. The only thing that seemed to help was going to my swing.

Dense gray swallowed every hint of color across the horizon. It was a perfect picture of how I felt inside.

I tried to turn my attention toward the Lord, but I couldn't seem to focus. I'd never had anxiety like this before, and if I did feel anxious for some reason, Bill had always been the steady one, able to level out my emotions. If there was a problem, he'd be there carrying the weight of responsibility. His constant encouragement to me was, "You're okay," and somehow, with his assurance, I knew I would be. Now I had to find my own "okay," and it was terrifying.

As I sat slowly rocking on my swing, the Lord drew my thoughts back to the story of David and and the heart-wrenching loss of Ziglag in the book of 1 Samuel. David and his company of 600 men were returning home. As they approached their village, Ziglag, to their horror, they discovered that a raiding band of Amalekites had attacked it, capturing their wives and children. Everything of any value was stolen and the village was burned to the ground. There was nothing left but the clothes on their backs.

I'm so grateful for the next verse: "Then David and the people that were with him lifted up their voice and wept, until they had no more power to weep," (1 Samuel 30:4, KJV).

Somehow in our culture we've gotten the idea that crying is a sign of weakness. Many widows have told me they stayed away from church in the beginning because they were afraid they would cry. Why do we apologize for our tears? Tears are healthy. They show the depth of the love we had for the one we lost. It's good to cry.

I love the New Living Translation of Psalm 56:8: "You keep track of all my sorrows. You have collected all my tears in your bottle. You have recorded each one in your book." Our tears are precious enough to God that He wants to save them.

It's what follows our tears that shows strength. I'm sure David and his men didn't shed a few dainty tears. They wailed until their strength was gone. But David was a leader, and amidst the tears, he had to make a choice: crumple or lead. He could have remained standing in the center of total brokenness, fixed on the devastation, but instead he chose to run to God.

" ... But David encouraged himself in the Lord," (1 Samuel 30:6b, KJV).

David called for the ephod. Calling for the ephod is the practice of putting on the garment of praise to worship God. The ephod was used by priests when they needed to seek God face-to-face. The closer we are to someone's face, the more it fills our view, and the less we can see of our surroundings. It's looking to God and nowhere else!

Originally, the ephod was worn only by the high priest. The Scripture says that Christ is our great High Priest (Hebrews 8:1-6). He stands face-to-face with His Father, making intercession on our behalf (Hebrews 7:15). The ephod represents Christ. When the priests put on their ephods, it was a symbol of putting on Christ.

David answered the anguish of his soul by remembering God's faithfulness. He sang. He wrote. He worshipped.

Perhaps this was when David wrote Psalm 34:1 "I will bless the Lord at all times; His praise shall continually be in my mouth." Perhaps he sang: "Hope in God, for I shall again praise Him for the help of His presence. O my God, my soul is in despair within me; therefore I remember You … " (Psalm 42:5-6a, NAS).

Many times, when I've been on the edge of despair, the Lord has whispered, "Tell me what you know to be true." He encourages me to remember, to recite the truth of His word, to put on the garment of praise. This is, in essence, what David did when he encouraged himself in the Lord.

This principle works for all of life's struggles. Every time we remind ourselves of who God is, a fresh deposit of hope is applied to our hearts. The challenge of a walk of faith is to keep our focus on the truth.

Psalm 34:3 tells us to magnify the Lord. Magnify means to "make great, or greater, to increase the dimensions of; to amplify." It means to "increase the importance of; to praise highly." [8] We can magnify the size of our problems or increase our awareness of God.

My grandson got a microscope for Christmas. He examined anything he could fit under the lens.

"Look at this, Mimmy," he said, refusing to tell me what I was about to look at. I took my glasses off and adjusted the lens til the object came into focus.

"Yuck! You didn't find that in my house, did you?"

"Mimmy, it's an ant head."

It looked like a monster, grim and ominous. But take the magnifying lens away, and it was insignificant in size.

When our problems appear ominous, we have to switch the focus onto God. When we remember how big God is, all our "monsters" start to shrink.

8) *Webster's Revised Unabridged Dictionary.* S.v. "Magnify." Springfield: C. & G. Merriam Co., 1913. Accessed at: http://gcide.gnu.org.ua/?q=magnify&define=Define&strategy=.

CHAPTER THIRTY-THREE

Tell Me What You See

There was a penetrating chill in the air as I tried to enjoy the swing one morning. The little quilt I had over my legs wasn't enough to keep me comfortable, so I gathered my things to go back inside. As I folded the quilt, a thought came across my mind:

Lift up your eyes. Tell Me what you see.

The warmth of the wood stove was calling me, but I paused for a moment and looked back at the barren hedgerow on the edge of our property. It was as grey and lifeless as before, a familiar late February scene in upstate New York. I saw nothing, so I dismissed the thought and reached down to the woodpile on the porch for a big log for the fire. Just before closing the door, I glanced back one more time.

A large whitetail deer was standing 20 yards from where I'd been sitting, right in the middle of that grey, lifeless hedgerow. I froze so as not to startle it. The deer didn't move; he cautiously listened. It was as if he wanted me to observe every glorious inch of his majestic frame. Then, he flipped his white tail and bounded off across the field, effortlessly leaping over every obstacle before he disappeared into the woods. *The deer must have been there the whole time hiding in those scrub trees*, I thought. *I almost missed this blessing because I thought I was seeing all there was to see.*

I love deer. Bill and I used to drive around at dusk and look for deer in the sprawling farmlands around our area. Seeing this deer tugged on good memories, memories I cherished. Glimpsing the deer in my yard was a very personal surprise from the Lord.

"There's more to My purposes than what you can see with your natural eyes," He whispered. "Within the folds of difficulty, I have hidden treasures, not from you, but for you: new deposits of grace, reminders of My love, and seed for tomorrow."

I closed the door and ran for my journal as 2 Corinthians 1:3-4 came to mind, "Blessed be the God and Father of our Lord Jesus Christ, the Father of mercies and God of all comfort, who comforts us in all our affliction so that we will be able to comfort those who are in any affliction with the comfort with which we ourselves are comforted by God" (NAS).

I thought back to the day I was taking a walk around our country block—about 4 miles. I was deep in thought and had my head down. Suddenly I heard someone say, "Did you see it?"

"See what," I answered, recognizing a neighbor.

"A huge buck just ran across the road 20 feet in front of you! Didn't you see him?"

"Aww, no, I had my head down."

"Too bad, he was a beauty."

I walked on home, miffed at myself for missing that. However, I sensed it happened for a reason. The Lord was telling me to keep my head up and my eyes lifted. Looking down leaves the journey uninspired.

165

Sometimes God has to open our eyes because we're so consumed with our burdens. When Elisha's servant saw enemy armies circling the city, he ran to Elisha in fear. Elisha said, "Do not fear, for those who are with us are more than those who are with them" (2 Kings 6:16, NAS).

Can't you just imagine the servant looking around in bewilderment? "Huh? Where? I don't see anyone on our side. All I can see is that we're in a world of trouble."

I can identify with that servant. But Elisha prayed. "O LORD, I pray, open his eyes that he may see. And the LORD opened the servant's eyes and he saw; and behold, the mountain was full of horses and chariots of fire all around Elisha." (2 Kings 6:18, NASB).

Sometimes grief is so overwhelming that God has to open our eyes, too. But He will, and when He does, it will help us to see His lovingkindness surrounding us.

As a widow, I felt abandoned by some of my friends, but I was still blessed by those God appointed to help me. They weren't the ones I expected—they were new friends, sent by God.

You've probably heard the phrase: "God doesn't waste our sorrows." But *how* does God redeem devastating loss? I could see nothing good about losing Bill. How *could* God turn this to good?

I didn't want to get swallowed up by grief. I didn't want to spend the rest of my life with my head down. I had to work at keeping my focus on God. It was not easy at first. It was a choice that took courage and more faith than I ever thought I would have. We never *get over* the loss of a loved one, but we learn how to live despite the loss. Part of God redeeming our loss is through the grace He gives us to keep going, keep living, keep looking at the blessings that remain. As I experienced the magnificent comfort of the Lord, a little more strength was deposited in my heart, and stories of encouragement were put in my hands. I could comfort someone else with the comfort I experienced. I called them my widow testimonies.

In one instance, I was returning home from the store with my four-year-old grandson, in Bamma's 1985 Oldsmobile, which I still drove at the time. That old car started choking and sputtering like it was about to die any minute. The temperature was over 90 degrees and very humid. I didn't own a cell phone. If the car died, walking with my grandson in that heat would have been dangerous.

"Okay, Lord, here's Your chance to prove Yourself strong for me. We need Your help. Please, get us home!"

The car coughed and jerked and sputtered along at about 20 miles an hour. This was a perfect opportunity to practice gratitude. So I kept thanking Him for His protection to widows. We had about six miles to go, but we made it. The car died 10 feet inside my driveway. The man next door saw my stalled car and came right over and fixed it. He'd never done anything like that before—I knew it was the Lord.

The next week, I had the opportunity to quiet the fears of a new widow with that story. This is one way our sorrows aren't wasted. With every touch of encouragement or hug of compassion, we are experiencing God in a personal way that fills our hands with more to give to others.

CHAPTER THIRTY-FOUR

Sick-and-No-Hairspray Isn't Pretty

I didn't realize how serious pneumonia was until I collected a few reactions from my friends:

"Oh, Nooooo!" I heard.

(Gasp.) "I'll pray."

Or, with a tone of great doom, "Uh-oh ... "

Then there was my mother-in-law's reaction: "I knew it! Marjorie, you're not drinking enough. You need tomato soup."

I got lots of advice: "You need to starve the fever," or "Be sure to eat." Then there were the extra remedies: put this essential oil on your wrists, this other oil in your navel ... (I've heard that peppermint oil dropped in the navel is supposed to bring down a fever.)

My favorite advice remains: Stay in your bathrobe for the next week and eat carbs.

Gone were the days of Bill's pampering. He used to be so attentive when I was sick—I loved it. In my mind, there's nothing worse than having the chills when you have to get up to find your own extra blanket.

"Marjorie, you're not as young as you think you are. I certainly hope you'll take care of yourself," said Bamma.

I wanted to say, *Aw, gee, really? I'm actually an idiot and I plan on going water skiing this afternoon if it stops snowing.*

It was fun answering the phone at the peak of laryngitis, when I'd have to clear my throat or cough between simple words. "Hel—(ahem)—lo-o ... ?"

Then the reply: "Marjeeee? Is that you?"

"No, it's my live-in boyfriend. Of course it's me. Who else would it be?"

"You sound sick? Are you sick?"

Sarcasm soars when I'm not feeling good. "Ya think?"

Of course, woe be to the telemarketer who got me off the couch: "May I speak to Mah-jor-ee Ste-hee-vahns?

"I'm sorry, Marjorie is no longer with us."

One thing I hate about being sick and alone is there's nobody to whine to. My friends are up to their eyeballs with life; they don't need me whining about a cold.

My mother-in-law repeated her instructions every time she got a glimpse of me. I'd even hear her yelling it from her end of the house. "You get sick because you do too much. You're getting old. You need to slow down."

The last thing I needed was to be lumped into the ready-for the-home bunch. She was 95. Of course I was doing too much in her eyes.

It isn't easy being alone when you are sick. Friends and family are compassionate, but from a safe distance. Who wants to visit when there's the risk of picking up your germy-glop? Bernice used to seal herself in her end of the house and drinks gallons of instant tomato soup.

Frankly, a few days of not caring how your hair looks can do a girl good. No hairspray suffusing the atmosphere for four whole days! (That's a good gauge for how sick I am.) Hair flying in reverse, black socks, a green sweatshirt with the hood up, bunched over a red plaid flannel nighty and a super fleece bathrobe on top of all of it ... lovely.

I was so sick one time, I put my bifocals on upside down and thought I was hallucinating.

Making chicken soup, even out of a can, takes more energy than reaching in the freezer for ice cream. I grab for all the wrong foods because who's cooking? I'm amazed my pancreas survives the infusion of carbohydrates consumed when I'm feeling sorry for myself. Who wants salad? All I can think of is crunchy-greasy-starchy *anything*, and more ice cream, of course. If I'm not going to be pampered by my husband, at least I can pamper myself with food.

I've heard people say, "I don't eat when I'm sick because nothing tastes good."

Unless I'm in a coma, food always tastes good to me. I've *never* lost my appetite. Even after enduring three hours of seasickness on a whale watch, I wanted to eat. The only time I stopped eating was when my jaw was swollen shut from having my wisdom teeth pulled. I still managed to suck down a chocolate milkshake.

I've found that food is not the only danger when I'm convalescing. It's best to hide my credit card, too. I'm more easily swayed. I'll go on Amazon to buy a book and see those little images at the bottom: "Customers who bought this item also bought ... " *Click*. One year I got all my Christmas shopping done before I finished a round of antibiotics, and I never left my house. That was a good thing ... except it was March.

The minute I feel better, I get the urge to organize. I sort through drawers and throw out a ton of stuff. As long as I don't have to get out of my bathrobe, or worry about my hair, I'm golden.

Nobody dares ask me to babysit, so I have a stretch of uninterrupted sorting time. Productivity is my happy pill.

I got a surprise visit from my neighbor, and when I opened the door, she jumped back, "Whoa! I sure hope you're sick ... because you look like hell!" (I love my earthy friend.)

"Hell-oo to you, too," I hacked, "I'm happy to finally see another human being."

"Well," she smirked. "It's probably a good thing you haven't. Sick-and-no-hairspray isn't pretty."

Aloneness can pack a nasty wallop when you are sick. I begin to look at the characters on *Law and Order* as family members. At least they have familiar faces.

I remember the first time I got really sick after Bill died. When I was finally feeling well enough to go outside on the swing, I opened the door and there on the little rug in front of me was a bright red and orange maple leaf.

I was puzzled because our leaves hadn't turned yet. Only the tippy tops of the maple tree were freckled with crimson. For a perfect leaf to flutter onto my porch and land in the center of my welcome rug defied probability.

I knew it was another widow testimony, an unsolicited encouragement from my God. *I see you, Lord.*

It felt better than a bouquet of flowers. Only God knows how the touch of autumn stirs my creativity. He knows I love to press leaves, and save them in my journal. To me, that maple leaf was a personalized "I love you."

The Bible says, "Many are the woes of the wicked, but the LORD's

unfailing love surrounds the man who trusts in Him"
(Psalm 32:10, NIV).

Are those touches merely a nice thought? Or are they truly tangible tokens of His unfailing love dotting our world? Is the expression of God's love merely isolated to a Bible verse or a Christian program? Are His expressions of love limited to the super-spiritual only? Can He show Himself in a leaf? With a deer? In a bird's song?

Psalm 86:17 says, "Show me a token for good; that they which hate me may see it, and be put to shame, because Thou, Jehovah, hast helped me, and comforted me" (NAS).

A token is a sign, a keepsake of relationship. It's little things that say, "I love you." Some may think it foolish, but the psalmist-warrior David didn't. Don't let your tokens of good be stolen. Look for them with child-like faith and expectation. It helps make the sick-and-no-hairspray times of life a little less dreary.

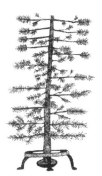

CHAPTER THIRTY-FIVE

The Square Christmas Tree

"I'm not going to decorate for Christmas," I told my friend as we wandered in our favorite country store. "Bamma says she doesn't care about a tree, and I always go to the kids' house on Christmas. Why bother? Bill won't be there to enjoy it." I picked up a shiny silver ball and looked at my reflection on the side. "What difference does it make?"

My friend was reveling in her cart full of country delights for her new home. She added a throw blanket to her basket, "This will be awesome around the base of my Christmas tree in the living room. Do you like it?" She turned, took one look at my face, and stopped rambling. "You have to decorate for Christmas. Want me to help?"

"This isn't working for me today. I think I want to go home."

"I'm done. I'll check out and meet you in the car." She handed me her car keys.

Once I got in the car, I burst into tears. *This is just too painful. Nothing is the same anymore.*

I heard the trunk open and close. She climbed in the front seat, "I'm excited about my new stuff … you have to decorate for Christmas" she said, starting the car. "Why not decorate your home for the Lord?"

This was going to be the second Christmas without Bill. The first year, I was only four months into widowhood and the holidays had been a total blur. I hoped this year would be different. "Come on, decorate the house for the grandkids. They don't want a sad Mimmy at Christmas," my friend coaxed.

The next day, I leaned the weathered step ladder up to the storage area above the garage. The minute I opened the door, a blast of memories came tumbling out. Bill's hunting equipment was piled on one side. I could see my mom's walker and my grandmother's sewing machine. On the other side was my dad's train set and a ship he built of wood. It had taken him almost a year to build.

I hoisted myself up into the storage space and sat in the middle of the cobwebs and musty boxes. It felt so strange to be submerged in the memories of so many loved ones knowing I'd never see them again this side of Heaven.

Saying goodbye to a loved one takes more than one funeral. It takes many funerals. Each memory includes a letting go, and another goodbye. Each piece has to be placed into God's hands.

The box of ornaments was right behind the artificial tree. As I pulled the box toward me, the side ripped and I caught a glimpse of the dreaded twinkle-light mess inside.

No matter how carefully I pack the lights each year, the minute I turn around, the twinkle-light demon, assigned to sabotage our yearly decorating experience, goes to work.

Coming in the door with my arms full, I heard Bernice. "Marjorie, you're doing too much. You won't be able to walk in the morning."

"Thanks for reminding me," I answered. "I'm going to take a rest now."

I grabbed a blanket and went to my beloved porch swing. Fresh snowflakes swirled in the air and it reminded me of our infamous square Christmas tree. One year, when our young sons were ages 10 and 12, my husband gave them the job of finding a Christmas tree in our back fields—the ultimate adventure. The next afternoon, Kyle and Jonathan rode the four-wheeler into the fields to accomplish their mission.

They were gone a long while. It had been lightly snowing when they left, but when they returned, it was snowing heavily. When I heard the roar of the engine coming over the hill, I was relieved. Around the corner of the garage they came dragging a huge heap of snowy branches behind the four-wheeler.

They were triumphant as they hoisted the tree up for my approval.

The thing was huge. It towered over us at least 10 feet tall, and defying all pine tree logic, was absolutely square! I guess my face said it all.

"Don't you like it, Mom?"

"Uh ... sure, wow. Only it's ... um ... *square.*"

"It's a Snoopy tree, Mom, It just needs a home."

It needed a home all right, but did it have to be mine? This was, by far, the ugliest Christmas tree I'd ever seen. The scant few pine needles fringed the tips of the branches. Pruning it into the right shape would leave us with sticks. Plus, we had to cut the top off to fit it inside the house, which made it even more square.

The tree left a trail of pine needles as we dragged it through the house. I would have waited for Bill's help, but the boys wanted it to be a surprise. They helped me anchor the beast in the old rusty tree stand, and then they disappeared.

Now I had a gargantuan, dysfunctional pine growth dominating the entire corner of the living room, plus a musty box full of tangled lights.

I tried hanging the lights in a triangular pattern, in hopes that, if you squinted at night, it would resemble a traditional pine tree.

Bill was due home any minute; the tree was ready to be unveiled as daddy's big surprise. I was not happy.

"Hey," I groaned as he walked through the door.

"What's the matter with you?" he said, kicking the snow off his shoes.

"I planned a surprise for you, but ... it didn't turn out."

Suddenly the boys came thundering down the stairs. "Dad, wait till you see the tree we got out back!" Kyle blurted out. "It's awesome!"

Bill didn't acknowledge the roll of my eyes as he walked past.

"Let's see, guys. Show me."

His reaction was what they'd hoped to get from me. Later I cornered Bill and whispered, "Tell me, what do you *really* think? Isn't it the ugliest tree you've ever seen?"

Bill looked at me bewildered, "It's just a tree."

It's just a tree! I chuckled as I remembered how mad I got at him for saying that. His answers were always so to-the-point and dry. Rarely did I get a compound sentence.

Sitting on my porch swing, I watched the giant snowflakes form little arching drifts between each spindle on the porch railing, and remembered what happened next.

Later that night, when everyone was asleep, I went into the living room for another look at the tree. I was very surprised to see it looked totally different as the twinkling lights took center stage over the shape of the tree.

Then a gentle question came into my mind. "What's the difference between this tree and a tree you would find in a king's palace?"

"The shape?" I whispered.

Thoughts kept coming, like sweet kisses on my speechless heart, far wiser than me, and I dared to believe He was saying:

This tree, growing wild in the field, is misshapen because it never had someone tend it. It never experienced the hands of a skillful gardener. Through Christ, you have been planted in the King's garden. Now My Master Gardener tends you with His watchful eye. He will prune away every wounded branch and lovingly tend and shape every new branch that grows. Stay rooted in Me, Child, and the promise of My fruitfulness will fill your branches.

That homely, square Christmas tree suddenly began to shimmer with even more radiance. It was the light *within* the tree that made it beautiful.

My eyes filled with tears as the memories of that special moment transcended time and space and became a word of comfort to my heart once again. *No matter how broken and misshapen I feel right now with Bill gone, I have a gentle Gardener tending me. Under His watchful eye, I can trust the future will be fruitful.*

Christmas might never be shaped quite the same without my husband, but it will always be rich, because it's the presence of His Light that makes life beautiful.

CHAPTER THIRTY-SIX

Declarations

I sat on my swing in the dark, and watched flashes of lightning blink across the sky. Within moments, wind streams shifted and tree limbs began to creak and groan. A foreboding storm crawled in across the valley threatening to own the night.

It started to pour. The rain began hitting my legs as the wind blew it across the porch, so I gathered my things to go inside. A great gust of wind slammed the door behind me. Bold streaks of lightning illuminated the kitchen windows, followed by deep growls of thunder.

The storm arrived so quickly, rain had blown in through the kitchen windows before I had a chance to close them. As I was wiping the water off the floor, the kitchen lights flickered and everything went dark. I stood there with an eerie feeling in the pit of my stomach. It was the first time the electricity had gone out since Bill died. By the time I fumbled around for matches and lit some candles, Bamma was yelling from her apartment. I quickly carried a candle into her room.

"Oh, I was worried you'd left," she said. Her little hair net had ridden up and was bunched on the top of her head. She was ready for bed and sat wrapped in her old burgundy bathrobe. The brand new bathrobe we bought her still hung in her closet. She insisted it was too nice to wear.

"I was out on the porch watching the storm roll in. Remember what I promised? I'll never leave the house without telling you first."

"It's a bad storm," she said, with a tremble in her voice. "Molly is afraid."

"We'll be fine, Molly, don't worry," I patted the dog, much to Bamma's approval. "The heat is off I'm going to look for flashlights. I'll be right back," I said handing her a lap blanket. But, before I could leave the room, there was an ear-splitting *crack!*

"What was that?" Bamma shrieked.

It was too dark to see except when the lightening flashed. I could see glimpses of a massive tree limb right outside the picture window.

"I think we've lost a big limb off the oak tree. It's hard to tell how big it actually is."

"Oh dear," she said, shaking her head. "If it's not one thing— it's another."

We sat and listened to more branches hitting the roof. Branches from the fallen limb now scraped against the side of the house. The whole house creaked with each gust of wind.

Bamma pulled the blanket around her shoulders. "The furnace is out, Molly is cold. She might get sick." I got the dog another blanket.

Lord, please protect us with these old trees.

Within a half-hour, the wind stopped and everything grew still. The rain slowed to a gentle patter against the roof. As quickly as it came, the storm was over.

Suddenly the lights flicked on. Bamma blew out her candle. "There now, Marjorie, you can stop worrying. It's over."

I chucked. "Okay, I'll stop worrying if you take that thing off your head. I don't know which is scarier."

She laughed.

"Do you remember the first time Jonathan saw you with your hairnet on? Remember he said, 'Bamma, you look just like Benjamin Franklin.'"

She nodded and patted Molly.

"It will take a while for the house to heat up. Are you sure you're warm enough?"

Bamma was already rooting around in her purse and didn't reply.

I turned the outside lights on so I could survey the damage in the backyard. Branches lay everywhere. I thought about how quickly the winds had shifted and how suddenly the storm approached. It made me think about how Bill went from a long-term illness to needing hospice care. We'd had warnings. We knew if God didn't intervene he would eventually die, but nothing prepared us for the day when the doctors announced there was nothing more they could do.

People told me I was blessed to know ahead of time that he was going to go. "At least it wasn't a shock," they said. But you are never prepared, no matter how much you know ahead of time. When the door of death slams, your whole world feels as if it's been knocked off its foundation.

The next morning I walked to the back of the house to see what had happened. It was a mess!

"This looks just how my life feels, Lord." I felt as if every part of me, all the plans and dreams for the future, lay broken and splintered like the branches in my yard. Death had whirled through our peaceful world and shattered everything.

As I surveyed the jungle of tree limbs and carefully stepped across the tangles, a verse came to mind. It was from Matthew 16 when Jesus asked Peter what people were saying about Him. Then Jesus asked, "Who do you say that I am?" (Matthew 16:15, NIV).

I knew He was asking me the same question. "You are my Lord" I answered, thinking about what those words really meant to me.

Something shifted inside me and I lifted my hands in worship.

"You are my Shepherd. You lead me. You are my song and the rejoicing of my heart. You will never leave me or forsake me. You are my comforter, My God, my ever-near companion. You hide me under the shadow of Your wings and surround me with Your unfailing love … "

As I declared out loud what I knew to be true, I could sense the Lord's pleasure and my despair began to lift. Though my feet remained in the same place, my focus was lifted above my circumstances.

"Father, I trust You in this. These are Your trees and I am Your daughter."

In my heart, I heard Him say, "Cling to Me, daughter. No storm can devastate you when you walk through it with Me."

When I turned to go inside, I saw Bernice watching from the window.

"What were you doing out there?" she asked as I came through the door.

"I was surrendering myself to whatever God has for me."

She stared at me for a moment and changed the subject. "Want some tomato soup?" (Instant tomato soup was her answer for anything that ails you.)

"No thanks."

"It's good for you," she countered.

"Oh, okay."

"This will make you feel better and you can finally stop worrying."

CHAPTER THIRTY-SEVEN

My God, My Rock

My son Kyle came over the following morning to look at the storm damage. I felt relief the minute he walked in.

"No problem, Mom. I'll have my guys take care of the yard."

"Oh, thank you so much," I exclaimed, throwing my arms around him.

Kyle's work crew came that afternoon. I'd tried doing a little cleanup myself, but what had been impossible for me was no problem to three young men with chain saws, wheelbarrows, and muscle. It only took them two hours.

As I watched them work, I imagined myself knee deep in the middle of all those broken branches. It's easy to get lost in the middle of so much brokenness. It's a much harder job than we realize.

Later that afternoon on the swing, I returned to Matthew 16:15 where Jesus asked Peter, "Who do you say that I am?"

Peter replied, "You are the Christ, the Son of the living God."

Jesus commended Peter, "Blessed are you, Simon son of Jonah! For this was not revealed to you by flesh and blood, but by My Father in heaven. And I tell you that you are Peter (petra), and on this rock (petros) I will build My church, and the gates of Hades shall not prevail against it" (Matthew 16:16-18, NIV).

Only in Matthew's account is the word "rock" used twice, but each use is actually a different Greek word. Petros means rock, or large stone, a detached, but large fragment of a larger rock ... "a size such as a man might be able to throw.[9]"

Petra, on the other hand, means a massive, living rock, a huge mass of rock rising up through the earth like a projecting cliff.[10,11]

A rock is not generally referred to as living—it doesn't breathe, eat, grow or reproduce. Rocks are objects. But it's no coincidence that the Holy Spirit inspired this word to be used. This paints such a beautiful picture: an immovable rock, towering with strength, but one that is also warm and responsive. Unlike the statues and graven images of false religion, our God is alive. And everything that comes from Him will be alive, too.

Jesus was preparing His disciples for what was ahead. He knew the challenges the church would face, and He was giving them keys to a strong foundation. He was telling them that natural strength can't be relied on. Idols cannot save you. Man-made religion is dead, not living. The kind of strength we need must come from a personal, revelational relationship with Christ, the Living Rock. There is no other way to build a strong life.

My thoughts flashed back to a special moment years ago when I was sitting outside reading John 12:24: " ... unless a kernel of wheat falls

9) "4074. Petros," HELPS™ Word-studies by Helps Ministries, Inc. Accessed at: http://biblehub.com/greek/4074.htm.

10, 11) "4073.Petra," THAYER'S GREEK LEXICON, Electronic Database, by Biblesoft, Inc. Accessed at: http://biblehub.com/greek/4073.htm.

to the ground and dies, it remains only a single seed. But if it dies, it produces many seeds" (NIV).

As I was writing my thoughts in my journal, suddenly a maple seed fluttered out of the sky and landed on my thumb.

What are the chances that a seed would fall on my hand at that exact moment? We had a maple tree, but it was far on the other side of the house.

Since I don't believe in coincidences, an excitement rose inside me. "Lord, help me understand." When I looked closely at what I thought was a maple seed, I made the startling discovery it was the wing off a dragonfly!

I recoiled and quickly shook the insect's body part off my thumb. These words sprang up in my heart:

Lord, I pray to know You so
That from my strengths I dare let go.
All natural ropes I grab to climb—let die
And there—my wings to find.

He wanted me to trust only in Him—not in my natural abilities, nor even my God-given talents. Only that which is built on a personal, living relationship with Christ will stand. Jesus modeled it in His own life when He said, " ... I tell you, the Son can do nothing by himself; he can do only what he sees his Father doing, because whatever the Father does the son also does" (John 5:19, NIV).

I pulled the blanket from the back of the swing and wrapped it around my shoulders. "Thank you, Lord, that You are my Living Rock. Thank you that I don't have to go through grief in my own strength."

CHAPTER THIRTY-EIGHT

The Ashes of Anxiety

As I ventured into my second and third year as a widow, things were definitely improving. I didn't cry every time I thought of Bill. Memories of him were sweeter, not so painful. I had a good routine and kept busy.

The household responsibilities weren't as overwhelming, either. I'd compiled a list of people I trusted to help with repairs and upkeep around the house. I learned to charge a car battery, and discard dead mice without freaking out.

I also felt the Lord nudging me to have the upstairs remodeled. It didn't make sense to me because I was sleeping in a bedroom downstairs. My budget was tight, but I followed His lead. A week after it was done, I got a phone call from a trusted friend, "Are you interested in renting a room or two?" A young woman from the local Bible college moved in that very week, and thus, my journey as a landlord began.

My first tenant stayed a year, then left to get married. Only a week later, the same friend called again.

"Is that student still living with you?" she asked.

"As a matter-of-fact, she just moved out."

"There's a young woman who needs a place right away."

"Wonderful," I replied.

In moved Susan, an emergency room nurse. Her mom had passed away when she was only 15, so she understood grief. We became good friends and I'd like to think I helped to fill a little of the hole in her heart for a mom. She was a godsend, and as a nurse, she was able to help me when Bamma got sick.

But there was one thing that hadn't moved out yet ... and that was my anxiety. I'd never had anything like this before. During the first year of widowhood, anxiety would come before making a big decision or doing something for the first time. Now it was different. This wasn't merely butterflies in my stomach. This anxiety was debilitating. It startled me out of a sound sleep in the mornings without any preceding thought or bad dream. It was a free-floating angst with a mind of its own.

Anxiety made me question everything about myself. Wasn't I the strong woman who'd travelled in ministry to many people, places and nations? If I was the woman who taught about prayer and worship, why couldn't I seem to pray this away? Why couldn't I overcome this anxiety? Should I have done something different? Was I losing my mind?

I wandered into Bernice's apartment before going to the swing one morning. She could see I was troubled.

"Sit down," she said softly. She listened to me describe my feelings. "It's loss, Marjorie. That's what it is. It will subside as you get your footing."

It was hard for me to believe that's what it was. I'd read about grief and attended a grief group for a while, but nothing was ever said about anxiety. I became increasingly convinced there was something really wrong with me, so I went to see my doctor. After a careful examination, she sat down.

"How long has it been now since your husband passed?"

"Almost two years," I said.

"I can see nothing physically wrong with you. I think this is a part of loss."

"That's just what my mother-in-law said, but it comes out of nowhere. It doesn't happen when I'm feeling sad. It seems to happen for no reason."

"You're still a new widow. It will take much longer than two years, and everybody processes grief differently," she said, picking up her things. "You were happily married for 40 years. Be good to yourself, and take all the time you need." She shook my hand and left.

I was almost disappointed there was nothing physically wrong. I'd hoped for a pill that would take it all away, but medication doesn't take grief away. Medication might help you sleep or help you with coping, but it won't eliminate the journey still ahead.

When I returned home, Bernice was waiting to hear about the doctor.

"Come and sit. How about some nice, hot, instant tomato soup?"

"I could have saved a trip to the doctor if I'd listened to you. She said the same thing you did … it's loss."

"Have some soup. It will make you feel better."

Even that sounded good. "Okay, I'll have some."

Bernice was happy. Giving me instant tomato soup was her way of helping. She got out of her chair on the second try and moved cautiously to the cupboard.

"I always say, there's nothing like a good cup of soup when you're feeling down."

She stood holding onto the counter and carefully watched my cup circling in the microwave.

"I don't know how we ever got along without these contraptions," she said as the microwave beeped. "Here now, don't burn yourself. This will make you feel better."

We talked a long time. I think it was the first time I realized what a gift she was. I thought I was *her* caregiver, but in many ways she was *my* caregiver, too.

That week, I came across a quote by author C.S. Lewis: "No one ever told me that grief felt so much like fear."

Knowing that anxiety was a normal part of grief was freeing. Now I needed to learn how to cope with it. I knew the porch swing was a sure seat in the Lord's classroom.

One morning, as I wrestled with a strong attack, I sensed the Lord directing me to 2 Timothy. Not sure what I would find, I started reading from the first chapter.

"... as I constantly remember you in my prayers night and day longing to see you, even as I recall your tears, so that I may be filled with joy. For I am mindful of the sincere faith within you ... For this reason I remind you to kindle afresh the gift of God which is in you through the laying on of my hands. For God has not given us a spirit of fear, but of power and love and a sound mind," (2 Timothy 1:6-7, NKJV).

How did Paul respond to Timothy's suffering?

First, he let him know he was praying. Widows really need to be remembered in our prayers. If a sister was in the hospital having her leg amputated, the church would pray through the operation, through the recovery, then pray and support her through the years of physical therapy as she learned to walk again. Losing a loved one is very similar to an amputation. The recovery is long and arduous. The widow has to learn how to live without the "leg" she depended upon.

Second, Paul encourages Timothy by reminding him of his sincere faith. This kind of edification is so important because even the strongest of Christians can question their faith in dark times. One of the greatest gifts you can give to someone is sincere encouragement.

Third, Paul acknowledged Timothy's grief and loss, then communicated his love for Timothy. "Recalling your tears, I long to see you, so that I might be filled with joy," (2 Timothy 1:4, NIV).

I had a few friends who showed me this kind of love and acceptance. I knew I could be very real with them, and they weren't going to be impatient or judgmental.

Paul goes on to give Timothy a loving reminder to help him stay strong. "For this reason, I remind you to fan into flame the gift of God, which is in you, "(2 Timothy 1:6, NIV).

This metaphor refers to stirring up the ashes in a smoldering fire. It means to relight.

When I burn logs in my wood stove, if there are any embers left after burning all night, all I have to do is stir them up, increase the airflow, add kindling and the fire will return to a nice steady blaze. The only time it won't rekindle is if the wood is buried in ashes I failed to remove.

Sometimes our "fire" starts to fade because we're overwhelmed with that which needs to be removed. I spent a lot of time on the swing repenting. I had to get rid of the anger and offenses I'd picked up because of how people treated me after Bill's death. I couldn't hold those things inside and expect my fire to be kindled.

I've read 2 Timothy a hundred times, but *this* time the Lord made it come alive, and I could feel Him stirring the embers in my heart.

Next, the Lord reminded me again of John 16:7 "But I tell you the truth, it is to your advantage that I (Jesus) go away; for if I do not go away, the Helper will not come to you; but if I go, I will send Him to you," (NASB).

Jesus called the Helper the Spirit of Truth, and stated that He would be a guide, speaking what he hears from God (John 16:12-13). Not only will He speak to us, the Bible says He will hold our hand and help us (Isaiah 41:13). He'll carry us on wings like an eagle (Deuteronomy 32:11). He will carry us like a shepherd carries a lamb, close to His bosom (Isaiah 63:9).

As believers, we are blessed to have the presence of this Helper with us. Too often we forget this, and drift into trying to do things in our own strength. Losing a loved one really magnifies our need to depend upon the Holy Spirit. Too often we forget He is here. But it's not communication with an unknown being somewhere above the clouds. We have a living person present with us at all times.

This is the greatest gift God has given us—Himself, in the person of the Holy Spirit. If we listen and depend on Him, how can we fail?

One morning, after a blast of anxiety, the Lord began to speak to me about not owning my fears and anxiety like property I had to be responsible for. *Turn it around, and make it a prayer for every widow, every hurting person going through loss.* I began to see the anxiety as a call to prayer instead of a burden to bear. This was an enormous step forward in the battle.

For the first year or two, I always sat at one end of the swing, as if unconsciously waiting for Bill to join me. As I progressed in my journey through grief, I suddenly realized one day I'd moved to the center of the swing. I hadn't realized I'd been waiting for Bill until I wasn't anymore.

It didn't occur to me that I had drifted from talking to my Helper until I found myself on the swing again one day, overwhelmed and in tears, unable to focus. I called a friend in desperation to talk to someone with skin on, but as it turned out, this friend was having her own crisis. I listened without telling her why I called, and then I encouraged her to release all her burdens to the Lord.

That's when I heard myself: I wasn't doing what I was telling her to do!

I returned to the porch swing with fresh determination to lift each care and fear.

Now when I purposely sit at one end of the swing, it's to make room for my spiritual Helper—the One sent alongside to guide me.

CHAPTER THIRTY-NINE

A Circle of Quiet

My swing sometimes makes the most irritating sound. It sounds like: *Rankle-irk. Rankle-irk.* It gets impossible to concentrate. So one day I decided to try my hand at fixing it. I dug around in the garage and found a can of WD-40 I'd watched my husband use on various hinges. I wasn't sure where to spray, so I just sprayed everything. It didn't work. *Rankle-irk. Rankle-irk.* Disgruntled, I cleaned up the drips, flopped on the swing, and decided to try my hand at being still.

Stillness doesn't come naturally to me. I always envied how my husband could sit motionless for hours and be thoroughly content, while I always felt a need to move or jiggle in some way. Bill could also go for hours without needing to say a single word, while I'd wake up talking. His response to my morning chatter was: "You have just used up my entire day's allotment of words and you're not even out of bed yet!"

I enjoy quiet, but it never made sense to me to be quiet when there was someone to talk to. I was quiet all day while he was at work, so by the time he got home I had a massive build-up of words. He'd come in the door, longing for quiet after spending the day with 100 high school freshmen and I'd barrage him with words. I had to learn that timing was *everything*. Chat-control was an art form I hadn't yet accomplished. (I'm still working on it).

I vividly remember one spring morning, probably 20 years ago, when Bill was sitting in his chair on the side porch peacefully enjoying the warmth of the sun on his face. I came bustling out the screen door with a flurry of chatter, totally oblivious to the special moment he was enjoying.

"Wow, have we got work to do today!" I announced.

He didn't respond to me. His eyes remained closed, he merely raised one eyebrow. Not taking the hint, I continued.

"We've *got* to do something about this porch! Look how the railings are peeling—it looks terrible!"

Bill silently shifted in his chair.

"Look at the weeds, they're taking over."

He shifted again, more deliberately this time, and cleared his throat.

"And look, the limb on that tree looks like it's going to drop any minute."

Finally, my patient husband could stand no more.

"Will you puh-leeeze be quiet? I don't know what you expect me to do: run for the porch paint, get the weed-wacker, or start up the chain saw. Let's just sit here together and enjoy the moment." Softening his tone, he continued, "I want you to try something. Turn off your engines, close your eyes, and simply *breathe*."

Some say men have a "think-nothing" place in their brains. I don't know if that's true. Whenever I asked my husband what he was thinking, and he said, "nothing," I just assumed what he really meant was "I don't want you to know," or "If I tell you, you'll give me your opinion and I don't want to have a big discussion right now, thank you." What I do know is that there is *no* such "nothing" place in my brain. My thoughts go 90 miles an hour. As a matter of fact, Bill used to say to me, "I don't know how you live with your brain."

"So explain to me how to turn my engines off?" I asked honestly.

He thought a minute. "I don't mean blank out your mind, that's not good. I mean place your thoughts on something, like the warmth of the sun on your face. Don't think about what you have to do that day. Don't analyze yourself. Just be still. Quiet your heart and let the peace of God rule in your thoughts."

The Lord was using my husband to teach me the art of being still. There's a big difference between quiet and being still. Our surroundings can be quiet, but our minds can be full of *rankle-irk* and worry.

The Scripture says, "Be still and know that I am God," (Psalm 46:10, NIV). That is not to be interpreted as wholly silent and inactive, but that we should not be fearful, nor fretful and impatient, or restless and tumultuous. Instead, we should be quiet and peaceful, resigned to the will of God.[12] It means to live with the posture of faith that God is in charge.

"How blessed the man you train, God, the woman you instruct in your Word, providing a circle of quiet within the clamor of evil...God will never walk away from His people," (Psalm 94:12-13, *The Message*).

A circle of quiet ... what a beautiful image. It's something we have to remember to step into. Stillness describes a quiet condition of the heart and a mental condition free of fear and worry so we can meditate on the Word of God. 1 Thessalonians 4:11 admonishes us to "make it (our)

---

12) "Psalm 46:10," *John Gill's Exposition of the Bible*. Accessed at: http://www.biblestudytools. com/commentaries/gills-exposition-of-the-bible/psalms-46-10.html

ambition to lead a quiet life: (we) should mind (our) own business and work with (our) hands ... so that (our) daily life may win the respect of outsiders and that (we) will not be dependent on anybody" (NIV).

There is much emphasis on meditation in the world of health today, but it is very different from Biblical meditation. The Bible doesn't encourage the type of meditation that is self-focused (looking inward). Biblical meditation is *God-focused.* It's looking upward, not inward. It's quieting our hearts, taking a posture of faith, and intentionally placing our thoughts on a Scripture verse or an aspect of His character.

The word "meditate" or "meditation" appears 20 times in the Bible. The definition of "meditate" in Strong's Exhaustive Concordance is: "to imagine, study, declare, speak, to murmur in pleasure, mutter, to ponder." I love that image of taking a Bible verse or passage and murmuring in pleasure to the Lord.

We are told to study Scripture, but in order for that study to take root in our hearts we need to *thoughtfully and intentionally reflect* on the Word, and even speak it aloud as a declaration. "This book of the law shall not depart from your mouth, but you shall meditate on it day and night, so that you may be careful to do according to all that is written in it; for then you will make your way prosperous, and then you will have success," (Joshua 1:8, ESV).

Have you ever watched coffee being made in an old-fashioned percolator, the kind with the little glass dome on top? The water boils in the bottom and then it bubbles up to the top so it can wash down over the coffee. The water is changed into something entirely different—coffee. And the longer it washes over the grounds, the stronger and richer the coffee becomes. That's what meditation is like: it's transforming.

When anxiety accompanied me like a deep wrinkle I couldn't smooth out, meditating on His Word helped transform my fears into a fresh focus. I'd sit on my swing, give God my worries and concerns, pray for others who might be suffering from anxiety too, then close my eyes, let the sunlight kiss my face, and murmur His sweet Words with pleasure.

CHAPTER FORTY

Loving Bernice

Grief makes us myopic. It turns our eyes inward. In the beginning, it's easy to become totally absorbed with grief. At first, my loss was all I could see. I viewed my world through the lenses of my grief.

I discovered how easy it was to become so focused on *my* pain that I lost sight of the fact that I wasn't the only one grieving in my house.

One day, Bernice said, "Marjorie, you seem to forget I *lost my son!*"

Her statement broke my heart. I'll never forget those words. They came like a sharp, corrective slap. My face flushed with embarrassment. Her stoic demeanor kept every tear privately locked away. She wasn't inclined to talk about her feelings—ever. It must have been hard for her to sit and listen to mine.

I apologized, but there was nothing more that I could say, so I retreated to the swing. Conviction grabbed at my heart. I knew if caring for my mother-in-law was where God had me, I needed to accept it and have a more loving attitude. I was too tense and short-fused. We were so different in the way we viewed life and the way we reacted to circumstances. I wore my heart on my sleeve and she kept hers locked up tight.

"You're quite difficult to live with, you know," she informed me one day.

How interesting that I'd been thinking the same about her!

This whole arrangement was a job for Jesus. I had much to learn. He began to give me bite-sized insights in *how* to love Bernice, with His help of course.

First, (proving God has a sense of humor) I had to let her feed me. She needed to feel that she was caring for me. That usually involved food, particularly her instant tomato soup, and often, grilled cheese sandwiches. My boys kidded Bamma about her "famous" sandwiches, which she made with fat-free processed "American" cheese slices, (which tasted like the plastic they were wrapped in), on white, fat-free bread, toasted to a crisp. My kids used to chase their friends around the yard, threatening them with those sandwiches.

Next, He showed me that she projected her feelings on the dog.

"Molly's heart is broken. Look at her, she's mourning."

I looked at Molly, lying peacefully in her very own, inherited blue recliner, sound asleep. She'd shown some sadness in the early weeks, but the dog was fine now. That led me to the second insight: *don't argue with her;* instead, agree with her.

"Poor Molly," I said. "But she'll pull out of this, don't you think?"

"You never get over it, Marjorie. You only learn to live with it. Look, she can barely go on."

Quickly I learned it was also my job *to be wrong.* I talked to a counselor about our struggles and she said, "Let her be right, even when she isn't. Unless it's harmful. She needs to feel as though she has some control in her life."

It was all about Bamma's dignity.

Swallowing your pride is never easy, even for the most humble among us, but I saw how miraculously it cleared the air and prevented arguments.

"Marjorie, what have you done with my pen?" she barked as she hobbled into the kitchen.

"I didn't take it, Bamma." Already I knew God was on the scene.

"Well, I guess a little bird took it." She turned to the dog and mumbled, "Your mother can't remember a thing."

Inside, I protested: *Why is it so easy to think I snuck into your apartment, stole your pen, and now I'm lying about it? Why would I want your pen? That's silly, I have dozens. Why can't you admit you misplaced it?* Thankfully, the Lord helped me keep my big, fat mouth shut.

"Let me help you look." *Lord, you're making me much nicer than I am.* I found it right away beside her chair.

"Here it is," I said holding up her pen.

"You can't have my pen, Marjorie, you'll have to get your own."

Fortunately, God helped me keep my sense of humor.

One day I was working at my desk when I suddenly I heard her shriek from her apartment. "MARJORIE! There's a leak! I hear water."

I came quickly, but before she saw me in the doorway, I heard her mumble to the dog, "Oh, it's the faucet. Your mother left the water on again."

I fought against being her caregiver. Between my mother, then my husband, I'd been caring for someone for 20 years. But this was where God had me, and I had to accept it. Matthew 25:40 says, "Truly, I say to you, to the extent that you did it to one of these brothers of Mine (and now my mother-in-law), even the least of them, you did it to Me" (NAS).

I had to let go of my will and believe if this was what God was asking of me, He would "equip (me) with every good thing to do His will," (Hebrews 13:21, NIV).

Bernice was a master at the art of acceptance. She often told me, "The Depression was worse than anything you kids had to go through. The government gave us food-rationing coupons. I had to save all my meat coupons so your husband could get protein. You do what you have to do, Marjorie, *without complaining.* Times were very tough, but it didn't help to cry about it. No one is going to cry with you, you know."

I wondered what untold history lay behind that last statement. She was tough, but life can break even the toughest. Bill and I were dating when he went into the military during the Vietnam War. I can remember Bernice standing at a distance watching us kiss goodbye. I wept as the bus pulled away. Her face was ashen as she stood frozen at the edge of the bus ramp, but I never saw her dab away one tear.

In later years, she nursed her husband through long, painful cancer, and when he died, she lived alone for more than 25 years. She *knew* what it meant to stand tough in difficult circumstances. I watched her keep her feelings private when she lost her sister, her brother, and her two best friends. She endured open heart surgery at 82, and worked with grit and tenacity until she regained her independence.

Bernice was 90 when Bill died. This she *couldn't* accept. She became frail almost overnight. "It isn't right. A child should *never* precede their parents."

Her steely resolve seemed to be dissipating. Though she never shed a tear in my presence and rarely complained, she wore her grief in other ways. She didn't stand as straight. She no longer resisted using her walker. Instead, she leaned heavily, drooping over it with increasing dependency.

She came down with her second case of shingles; she'd had it once before, after her husband died. I noticed the heating pad was out regularly and she needed Tylenol every morning to manage pain between her shoulders. She didn't putter around her apartment as she once did. But she still resisted my help with all her might.

"Bamma, would you like me to discard the junk mail for you?"

"Don't touch it, Marjorie. I have to shred it so no one gets my address." Instead, ads and newspapers piled high.

Most days she sat staring out the window. I worried she wasn't getting good nutrition because she ate the same things everyday.

"Bernice, would you like me to make your dinner for you?"

"Marjorie, you don't have to wait on me. You have to let me do it myself," she insisted.

"How about we share my leftover chicken?"

This seemed easier to accept for some reason. So we ate together that night.

"Molly loves chicken," she said, as she cut small pieces and saved them carefully on the side of her plate. Bernice mostly ate frozen dinners, provided they didn't have more than 4 grams of fat. Then she'd save all the meat for Molly.

Any attempt to talk about vitamins or better food choices was off limits. It was apparently none of my business. I learned that suggestions like that had to come from anyone else but me.

It took us several years to find the rhythm of living together, but we did. We became good friends, and though the words "I love you" were never spoken, deep love was there.

"Marjorie, do you want some instant tomato soup? It's good for you."

"Sure," I answered with a smile. "That would be lovely."

CHAPTER FORTY-ONE

Handle of Hope

My swing continued to be my healing place. Even in the coldest weather. I dragged out Bill's sleeping bag and sat in it so the wind wouldn't
freeze my legs.

I bought a baby monitor and carried it wherever I went in the house. I never told Bamma I could hear her talking to herself. It was more important that I could hear if she called.

"I'm going on the porch for a little while, Bamma. Will you be all right? I have the monitor with me so you can call for any reason. I'll come right away."

"Marjorie, you're too old to sit in the cold. You'll catch your death."

I don't know what I would have done without the Lord and my swing. Just knowing He was always there for me, helping me, giving me grace for each day. I sincerely wanted to take care of Bernice, but it was becoming a bigger assignment than I ever knew it would be. Bill had been gone for five years now. Being a caregiver, even for someone you love, is tough, and compounded my feelings of brokenness. Every day it was a struggle to remember God had a plan and that He was shaping every broken piece of my heart into something for His glory.

One morning, as I soaked in the quiet, a clear memory came to mind. I was a freshman in the arts program at R.I.T and used to take the bus into the city campus. Sometimes, when the seats were all taken, people had to stand and hold on to the straps that hung down from the ceiling. When the bus turned a corner, you would sway, but if you held on tight you wouldn't fall.

I clearly remembered seeing my reflection in the bus windows as I stood one night on my ride home from class. A young woman with long blonde hair, her whole life ahead of her, holding on to the bus strap with one arm and balancing a large drawing board under the other arm. An engagement ring sparkled on her left hand. I was going to be a great artist, I would marry Bill, and we would be together forever.

It seemed odd to be reminded of this, but then the Lord whispered, "I am your handle of hope."

I knew exactly what He meant. Just like the strap on the bus that would keep me from falling, I could hold on to Him and He would support me through the dips and turns of life. All I had to do was reach up in faith, and hold on tight to the One who would never leave me or forsake me.

I saw Bernice in a different light when I came back inside. I was, in many ways, *her* handle of hope. I was the immediate person she had to hold on to, which was a change for this staunch, independent woman who hated being dependent on anyone. She was grateful, and often told me so, but giving up her independence, and losing her only child, was a storm far beyond her strength.

"Feel better?" she said.

"I love my swing," I answered, rolling up my sleeping bag.

"You're crazy," she teased. "Would you make me some instant tomato soup and join me for a cup? Be gentle with my microwave—you might break it."

Her comment rolled off me. "Bamma, do you remember the handles on the bus for people without a seat?" I asked.

"Of course."

"Well, the Lord showed me that our faith is like that handle. When times are really hard, all we have to do is reach up to God and He will steady us."

Bernice was quiet.

"Isn't that encouraging?" I asked.

Her answer surprised me. After a long pause she said, "Marjorie, you are a strong woman. Bill would be very proud."

Her encouragement meant the world to me, and I got a bit choked up. Bernice's faith was rich, but very private. Several times I'd be about to walk in her room and I'd see her with her rosary. She wasn't comfortable talking about the Lord. I'd like to believe that our talks helped enrich her experience with Him as they did mine. I shared all the little lessons and pictures He gave me. I could see how His love was growing between us. Our differences didn't matter as much.

The Lord kept giving me fresh revelations for each stage of grief. The handle of hope was my illustration for this next stretch of time. Often, I'd simply raise my hand in the air and grab that invisible handle for the strength to continue. When I had no words to pray, I'd just reach for His handle of Hope.

CHAPTER FORTY-TWO

The Fall

Bamma had developed open sores on one foot from poor circulation, though she didn't have diabetes. The sores became infected, but she insisted on taking care of them herself. We went to the doctor twice, but the antibiotics prescribed weren't helping.

The doctor recommended a visiting nurse, but that was only for an hour in the mornings. The rest of the time I handled the wound care. Bamma's leg swelled so much that water dripped through the pores of her skin. I changed her dressings 8 to10 times a day. She was instructed to keep her legs elevated, but she kept forgetting. Her resistance to my reminders made things impossible.

"Bamma, you have to keep your legs up."

"I am, see?" she lifted her foot a few inches off the footrest on the chair.

"This problem is too great to handle at home, even with the extra help from your nurse. I really think you need to be in the hospital," I said.

"No-no-NO! I won't go," she yelled, her eyes wide with fear. "People

DIE there!"

She could barely walk with her walker. We didn't have a wheelchair, so getting her to the car was impossible.

"I'm sorry Bamma, you have to go. I've called the ambulance. It's on the way."

She was furious with me. "You move too FAST. That is NOT a good TRAIT, Marjorie."

Kyle arrived as the ambulance crew carried her out. "She's very upset with me, but I didn't know what else to do."

"You did right, Mom," he said. He took charge, following the ambulance to the hospital.

It wasn't until after they were gone that I fell apart. *Did I do the right thing? How long is this going to continue? What if she gets worse, or loses her leg? I can't do this anymore.*

I felt enormous relief as I watched them back down the driveway. She would get the care she needed, Kyle would handle everything, and I could catch my breath.

I decided to clean her apartment—something she would *never* have allowed me to do.

I felt a huge weight lift off my shoulders. I was free from the responsibility, free of the stress. And though I loved her, I secretly hoped they'd recommend a nursing home.

Bamma's room was dotted with tissue boxes and stacks of sterile bandages. First I removed every curtain and opened all the windows for the first time in years. Then I ripped off the black plastic bags taped over the footrest of her chair. Next, I found her mug and set it in hot soapy water and bleach to lift months of coffee, tea and instant tomato soup stains.

On the night stand was her hair net, a flashlight, Pepto-Bismol, and a statue of Mary. Her rosary beads lay twined on the bureau scarf and I made a mental note to take them with me to the hospital that evening. Over the next few days, I washed her collection of antique glass. I'd offered before, but she'd always insisted I'd break something. The colored glass twinkled with sunlight as I washed off months of dust and placed them back on the wide window sills we'd built seven inches deep to hold her collection.

I washed everything, tossed out dozens of random rubber bands and paper clips. I threw out a year's worth of advertisements and junk mail she planned to shred for fear of throwing anything in the trash with her address on it. I respectfully shredded the addressed pages and threw the rest in the garbage.

I shampooed her chair, washed her bedding, and all the curtains, then boxed all the medical stuff and put it in the closet.

While in the hospital, Bamma contracted two serious, hospital-borne infections. The odds of her recovery appeared very slim.

I learned with my own mother how important it was to have an advocate. Bernice didn't agree. She told me I was being pushy, bossy, or meddling. But I finally convinced her another set of ears wasn't a bad idea.

"Well, if you insist, you can be here when the doctor comes in, but *don't* say anything."

I had to promise. I soon discovered that what she heard was often quite different from what I heard.

"Bamma, the doctor said you were supposed to ... "

"He NEVER said that. You're WRONG."

Fortunately, when Kyle said he heard something, she believed him. It was becoming clear that her grandson was the one she wanted to be her advocate. It hurt my feelings at first, but then I came to my senses that

God was providing me with some relief.

Ten days later, the leg infection was under control so that she could be sent to a rehabilitation facility for extended recovery. She stayed there for three months.

It was the first time in 43 years that I was alone in the house. It felt very empty, yet strangely wonderful at the same time. I felt free of the heavy responsibility and isolation that came with her care, and for the next three months, I focused on caring for myself.

Bamma seemed very weak, and still had the bacteria she'd picked up in the hospital called Clostridium Difficile, or C. diff. I was shocked when the doctor announced that they were sending her home.

"What?" I said in amazement. "Doesn't she still have C.diff? Will my family be at risk?"

"There shouldn't be any risk."

"Does that mean there isn't, or hopefully not? Psychologically, I'm not ready for this," I told him with tears in my eyes. "My husband died not too long ago and I'm trying to get my life back and … "

"I'm sorry, Mrs. Stevens, I know it's hard, but we can't keep her here anymore. You'll have to talk to the social worker."

I cried all the way home. The ambulance would be coming in only a few hours. *God, I can't handle this. I don't want to handle this.* The pit of anxiety in my stomach was debilitating, and made it hard to breathe. How could I honor the promise Bill made to his mom if I fell apart?

I went to the porch swing and tried to envision reaching for that handle of hope. It wasn't there. I searched my heart for that circle of quiet, that hiding place in His arms, but every inspiration seemed to elude me. I didn't feel God's comfort. All I felt was an overwhelming tidal wave of grief. *This is not what I wanted my life to be. I don't want to live without Bill. I don't want to be on my own. The weight of it all is too much, Lord, where are You?*

Only one thought came to my mind. I remembered the day Jonathan and I were talking in the kitchen. I was stirring something on the stove while he leaned against the kitchen counter and listened to me express my frustration over the loss of my voice. After a long pause, Jon simply said, "Mom, you either trust God, or you don't."

Comfort was not what I needed. I needed to challenge my faith like Jon had that day. This was where God had me, so He would give me the grace I needed to get through.

When they wheeled her in and I saw how utterly helpless she was, I was worried. *Lord, please, please help me. I can't do this without You.* The next day, the visiting nurse came. When I saw who it was, I was overjoyed. God had sent a good friend I'd known years ago. We'd lost touch, and in the meantime, she'd become a nurse. We threw our arms around each other.

"God knew I needed a friend. It's so good to see you."

Bamma liked her, too.

I looked forward to her coming each day. After she cared for Bamma, we'd go outside on the porch and talk. I so missed having someone to air my daily concerns. It was the hardest part of losing Bill. God knew how much I needed her. She had a tender, loving heart. She didn't preach, advise, or correct. She understood, as a professional, the load I was carrying, and kept encouraging me. Just a few minutes with her made me feel so much lighter.

"This really is a job for more than one person," she told me.

"Thank you for saying that," I replied, choking back the tears.

Bernice never should have come home. She wasn't ready. She still needed far more care than one hour from a visiting nurse. I was trying, but it was too much.

Bernice had only been home for a few days when she had another terrible fall.

She was hurrying to the bathroom when she suddenly felt faint. She tried to get to her bed, but she passed out and fell, hitting her head on the sharp edge of the hardwood footboard.

Even though I had the baby monitor next to me, I was so exhausted I slept right through the crash and her initial cries for help. She was on the floor for almost two hours before I finally woke up. I went running into her apartment to find her lying in an eight-foot circle of blood and excrement. Blood was smeared up the wall and on the closet doors. She'd been flailing around banging on the walls to get my attention. The emergency necklace hung around her neck, but she had never pushed the button.

"GET ME UP!" she yelled.

"No, Bernice, I don't want to move you. I'm calling the ambulance."

"No, no! Don't call them. Just get me up." She was obviously in shock.

I called Kyle immediately and he came right away. I tried to pull up her slacks to give her some dignity, but they were too twisted and I couldn't move them

Bamma quieted down at the sound of Kyle's voice. He rode in the ambulance with Bernice while I was to follow soon in my car.

I returned to where she'd fallen and surveyed the horror. It looked like a crime scene. It never occurred to me that there were agencies for hire that cleaned sites ravaged like this. In shock myself, I just dropped to my knees and started to clean it up. It took me weeks to get over the trauma, and simply walking into her apartment could trigger the memory of those smells. No one else smelled it but me.

Again Bamma was sent to rehabilitation. We thought for sure she would never recover from such a violent head injury ... but she did!

CHAPTER FORTY-THREE

Life-Theme Reignited

After her latest fall Bernice stayed in rehabilitation for only a month. While she was gone, I had a chance to retreat from the stress of caregiving. I spent time reading old journals and even dared to read some of Bill's diaries. I came across love letters from our courtship. Sweeter tears flowed this time—not tears of grief, but tears of gratitude for the blessings and tender moments we had shared.

I've always had a life-theme. A life-theme represents a personal quest, something you are always searching for. Bill's life-theme was to live orderly, peacefully, and close to Him. Mine was to always be watching for signs of God's unfailing love.

A dear friend of mine, now deceased, taught me years ago to look for God's unfailing love in every detail of life. Walter had cerebral palsy, like my brother George. That's probably what drew me to him at first. We met at a fellowship coffee house in a nearby town. It was open to everyone and not affiliated with any particular church. We became instant friends. Walter had been a patent attorney, but his increasing physical challenges made it necessary to retire early.

Walter had no family nearby, only a sister living in Hawaii. He lived alone. He was very poor, but lived a rich life with God. He was a student of the Word, and a faithful intercessor in prayer.

Our relationship was primarily over the telephone. On occasion, Bill and I invited him to come for dinner. Our house was a bit too noisy for Walter, and most of our furniture was uncomfortable for his condition, so he never stayed very long. He carried an adjustable lounge chair so he could lie down and prop his legs up on pillows.

Walter loved to bring slides taken from nature. I'd drag out our old projector and we'd shine the pictures on our wall.

"What Scriptures do you see represented in this picture?" he'd ask.

At first, I saw nothing, but in time, I began to see principles of God's truth that were hidden in every picture.

"See the bud beside the autumn leaf?" he pointed to a branch in the fall. "That bud is the promise of new life to follow. During seasons of difficulty, like winter, when everything appears to be dead, we can know by looking at that tiny bud nestled beside the dead leaf, that new life *will* come. All of nature sings of the glory of God," he said, "you just have to keep looking."

My spiritual life grew because of Walter. He trained my eyes to see beyond the surface of things and to constantly look for God's treasures. It kept me living in the moment, and watchful. My heart was focused on the Word, and my eyes were on the Lord. During this season, I wrote my greatest volume of songs. One little chorus expresses it well:

Jesus In My Eyes
Listening to the breezes in the daytime,
Catching twinkles from a starry sky,

All I am and all I ever will be
Comes in love from everything around.
Life goes on in endless repetition,
Colorless to those who cannot see.
All the special things that come in living,
Hidden treasures in the little things.

Chorus
Spirit's lullaby, gentle songs of life.
Love's light surprise,
Jesus in my eyes.

© 1980 MARJI STEVENS

Walter's influence helped me through grief. My classroom was my porch swing. The sunrise became my daily reminder that God never changes. My teacher was the blessed Holy Spirit. All I had to bring to God was my naked self. All I could do was place the broken pieces of my heart into His hands and watch Him shape a miracle.

I listened with new anticipation to hear the Lord's whispers. I watched with an eye of expectancy. I looked for God's Truth in every leaf and blade. The rain reminded me of Isaiah 35:6: "For I will pour out water on the thirsty land, and streams on the dry ground; I will pour out My spirit on your offspring, and My blessing on your descendants" (NIV).

I had to believe and declare these promises to myself: I *will* have water for dry ground, streams *will* pour forth, my wilderness *will* run with an abundance of water, because God is a God of restoration.

Sitting on my swing, watching stark, black branches silhouetted across the salmon evening sky, I was wooed to persevere through the last stretch of winter. Lime green buds in the smoke bush beside the porch heralded new life coming to kiss the earth.

Only believe daughter. New life is coming for you, too. You can count on it.

A red cardinal reminded me of the blood of Christ. *I paid the price ... I purchased your freedom.* Azure skies testified of Heaven's touch of blue. The life-theme of God's unfailing love stretched out in evening's sunlight, fingering the ground. The wind announced His coming: "Look! Here he comes, leaping across the mountains, bounding over the hills," (Song of Solomon 2:8, NIV).

Widowhood was not the end of my life; it was not the end of my dreams. Yes, I would always miss Bill, but this was a new beginning for me. This next season of life would be just as adventuresome as the former season, because of the One I follow.

Part of His miracle was letting me see that my true gift had never really been lost or damaged. I had believed God gave me the gift of music, but now I could see that music was only a part of His greater gift: *creativity.* Even in the darkest times I never lost creativity.

Despite Bill's death, my mind was bursting with ideas. Over the course of several months, I created the illustrations for a new children's book: *The Little Clock That Couldn't Tock.* Next came the Baby Moose series, inspired by my first grandson, Owen: *Baby Moose and the Shiny Red Fireman Hat, Baby Moose Learns to Go Potty,* and *Baby Moose in Blahville.* After that, another grandson, Everett, inspired *Everett and the Big Fat Chicken,* while my granddaughter Hazel inspired *Is That My Bus?*

I also joined a Christian writer's critique group, built a website, and began to blog regularly. I wrote about my journey through loss, and the joyful rhythm of a Spirit-led life.

One morning on the swing, my spirit leapt as I read Isaiah 35:6: "... The tongue of the mute will shout for joy, for waters will break forth in the wilderness, and streams in the desert," (NASB).

The name Judah means praise. *Could it be that the brooks of song will flow through me again? Could it be that the long-forgotten joy of singing will return? Lord, do I dare approach this buried dream?*

For the first time, after burying the loss of my voice, a prayer formed in my heart: "God, please restore my song."

God was reigniting my life-theme. I decided to study more about it. The Hebrew word for unfailing is *anekleiptos,* it's a combination of "a," meaning *"not"* and *ekleipo,* *"to fail*—or *not* left behind," describing something that will not give out, cease, or fail to perform.[13] Applying the synonyms showed me that His love is *constant, dependable, endless* and *unfading.* Further, His love is *inexhaustible, boundless, tireless,* and *ceaseless.*

Meditating on this truth was healing to my heart and brought wonderful memories. I remembered the first time the Lord emphasized His *unfailing* love. It was a few months after my Dad died. I had a ministry engagement at a retreat center about two hours from my home.

Unfortunately, my usual travel companion was unable to go. I was still struggling about the loss of my Dad and felt a bit timid about going alone, so I sought the Lord for a verse to hold on to. He gave me this one: "Many are the woes of the wicked, but the LORD's unfailing love surrounds the one who trusts in Him" (Psalm 32:10, NIV).

It was comforting, but I wondered what His *unfailing love* would look like. Was it only an invisible truth to cling to by faith? Or would I actually be able to see it? I sensed Him telling me to *look* for signs of His unfailing love. He didn't explain what they would look like, only that I should be watching.

---

13) "413.Anakleiptos," *HELPS™ Word-studies by Helps Ministries, Inc.* Accessed at: http://bible-hub.com/greek/413.htm

I'd been to this particular conference center a dozen times, but somehow I missed the highway exit. I decided I'd take the next one and double back on the country roads, but instead I got lost. My lack of confidence soon swelled and anxiety twisted in my stomach.

I was relieved when I came to a little berg with a gas station and convenience store. I pulled in next to another car and noticed a man sitting behind the steering wheel, drinking a root beer. He looked like a cross between my father and the actor Ernest Borgnine.

I rolled down my window, "Excuse me, sir, can you tell me how to get to Watson Homestead?"

He smiled broadly. "Sure, you go down to the corner and take a left, then take your next right. You'll want to follow that road and take the second left ... "

My eyes glazed over. I was too embarrassed to admit I didn't catch anything past the first turn. I thanked him and headed out again—clueless. I even got the first turn wrong. Instead of taking a left, I went right. Suddenly, I heard a honk behind me. I looked in the rearview mirror and saw the man had followed me. He signaled to turn the other direction.

At the next turn, I went the wrong way again. *Honk, Honk!* He was still behind me. A bit nervous, I locked the car door before pulling over to the side of the road. He drove up beside me and rolled down his window.

"Follow me," he called out, chuckling with amusement. Relieved by the laughter, I decided to follow him.
To my surprise, he not only took me back to the highway, he drove the next 10 minutes to the correct exit. I was almost in tears thanking the Lord for sending this man to help.

As he turned to go on his way, he stuck his hand out the window and waved, but it wasn't a usual wave. He held his hand still and bent his fingers up and down *exactly the way my father used to wave.*

216

I gasped, "Lord, that's just like my dad."

Then I heard the Lord whisper, "I will surround you with My unfailing love."

Tears of gratitude poured down my cheeks as I turned into the driveway of the conference center and found the building I thought was the right one. After unloading the sound system, all the inventory I sell, and my suitcase, a young woman appeared.

"Excuse me, but I think you might have the wrong building," she said. Sure enough, ours was down the road.

My heart sank. But coming in the door behind her, I heard a familiar voice, "Hi Marji, need some help?"

Three old friends rushed up to hug me. "So sorry to hear about your dad. We're here to be a blessing."

They helped me reload my car and then they carried all the equipment into the right building.

"My unfailing love," He whispered.

The retreat was a blessed time, and the fresh message of God's unfailing love proved to be just what we all needed.

Years later, the theme of His unfailing love still comforts me as I look for the daily blessings that cross my path: the chickadee that suddenly appears on the porch railing, a peony shoot pushing through the spring snow, a surprise phone call from a friend when I'm feeling lonesome. It's such a joy to see the simple, daily ways in which He reveals His amazing, unfailing love.

"Yet hope returns when I remember this one thing: the Lord's unfailing love and mercy still continue, fresh as the morning, as sure as the sunrise. The Lord is all I have, and so in him I put my hope," (Lamentations 3:21-24, GNT).

217

CHAPTER FORTY-FOUR

Avoidance

Can we talk underwear for a minute? At the risk of being totally transparent here, I put off bra shopping until it's an emergency. It's such a hassle trying them on in the store, and I refuse to have a clerk helping me with the right fit. A bra is the last thing I want to spend $40 or $50 dollars on. In my mind, it's like sinking money into a new septic tank that you're going to bury in the ground. All my bras are wearing thin, especially the fabric that holds the underwire. It's probably my fault because I don't bother with the delicate cycle. I throw them in the washing machine with all the towels and jeans.

I used to care what my bras look like, but now that I'm alone, I'm tempted to think *why bother?*

My friend called one day, all excited that an expensive lingerie store at the mall was having a huge sale. "You can get their to-die-for panties for only $10 a pair."

"For only one?" I questioned. "I usually get a package of six nice, white ones for that price."

"You really should treat yourself once in awhile. It's good for you," she countered. I have no trouble treating myself, but in my mind, buying underwear does not classify as a treat.

Well, my refusal to deal with old, unruly underwires backfired while I chatted with a woman at a dressy affair. I was admiring her stunning, light blue suit when suddenly ... *pinch-STAB-YEOW!* The fabric holding in the underwire on my bra gave way, giving me a nasty poke. The stab was so sharp my arm rocketed out in front of me and my teacup and muffin launched into the poor lady's elegant lap!

"Oh, I'm so sorry! My bra suddenly poked ... " My pathetic apology went unnoticed because she disappeared into the ladies room.

What possessed me to even keep that fraying bra? Did I think the fabric would somehow heal itself if I ignored the problem and stuffed it back in the drawer? I was postponing the dreaded task of bra shopping. Go figure.

This kind of avoidance is certainly harmless (except for the lady with the light blue suit) but avoidance of grief *can* be harmful. Avoidance is the desire to block out what we need to face, or keep away from something that is uncomfortable or unpleasant when we're meant to face it.

Perhaps avoidance is the reason our churches are weak in caring for widows. Death is inconvenient. It forces us to look at things we don't want to think about. It disrupts our peaceful world. It presents questions we can't answer. It's messy. We want to look away, tiptoe past the discomfort, keep focused on what makes us happy. This too often leaves the person in grief standing alone.

Grief doesn't go away fast enough for most onlookers. So we send cards and casseroles, but months down the road, when grief gets the toughest, most people have moved on. Your crisis of loss becomes old news, and once again, you, the person in grief, are left standing alone.

I'm guilty myself. Years ago, an acquaintance of mine lost a son in a tragic car accident. Her boy was the same age as one of mine at the time. I cringed every time I saw her. Not because I didn't care about the woman, but because my mind raced to what-ifs. *What if that was my son?*

I'm ashamed to say I avoided her. It was fear that kept me away. A single card was the best I could do. Then one day, the Lord convicted me that I needed to face what I was avoiding, so I invited her to meet me for lunch. (I should have offered to pick her up). I remember her posture at the table as her shoulders dropped from the weight of her brokenness. It crushed my heart. Finally, I gathered the courage to be honest. I told her my reaction to her loss. I could see a brief rise of anger in her eyes but it yielded to gracious forgiveness as I told her how sorry I was.

"The thought of losing my own son paralyzed me with fear. I didn't know what to say and I had no courage to face you."

She listened, but I'll never forget what she said: "I'd rather you say the wrong thing than to say nothing at all."

What started as selfishness became seeds of later ministry, graciously watered by her forgiveness.

I also avoided my own mother. I avoided facing our history, our mechanical politeness, void of the ability to confront issues we should have discussed. I avoided the grieving woman left a widow at 56, with a multiply disabled teenage son, because I didn't know how to push my own grief aside to be there for her. Later, when death removed the love of my life, I understood, and I wept for the things I could have done.

Avoidance can rob you of wonderful blessings. There were many things I avoided as a new widow, certain areas of the house, places we used to go together. Bill and I used to enjoy one secluded place on

Canadice Lake in the Finger Lakes. We'd go for an afternoon in the summer. He'd fish. I'd write. I avoided going there for years.

One day, I realized I was robbing myself of a beautiful day trip, so I bundled up a couple of grandkids and went. I was amazed to find the same spot. It felt so good to be there. I found the same gnarly tree where we used to sit and dangle our feet over the water. I was so glad I'd stopped avoiding it out of fear of stirring up grief. It made me feel a little sad at first, but that shadow quickly dissipated into a lovely afternoon.

I remember being overwhelmed when I surveyed Bill's 60-year collection of fly fishing, deer hunting, and archery equipment. Every piece came with a memory attached. I used to sit on a pile of boxes in the corner of the garage and watch him reload shotgun shells. I remember the rhythmic sounds of the reloader, the pungent smells of gunpowder and solvents, the satisfying feeling of watching him work. For a long time, I avoided going into the garage because I couldn't face the wave of grief sure to be waiting there. I knew that every piece would require a decision. *Who should I give this to? What should I sell? What can be tossed away?* It was not easy to do, but afterwards I had a wonderful sense of accomplishment. The crawl-space giant had been faced—and I felt clean inside.

I avoided going back to the little church, not much bigger than a home group, that my husband had loved. All I could think of was that he wasn't sitting beside me. This church had welcomed Bill's newly acquired interest in the electric bass. He joined the worship team even though he'd only taken two lessons. They didn't care if he faked half the songs. It was *home,* and I guess you know you're home when you don't have to worry about impressing anyone. You can just be yourself. After Bill died, I told myself it was too far to drive. There was always some excuse for not going, but I was avoiding going alone. When one of my sons asked me to accompany him to his church, I started attending a Sunday service again.

Sometimes people avoid going to familiar places out of fear that they'll become emotional in public. One time I burst out in tears at the grocery store just because I passed Bill's favorite pickles on the shelf. I used to be afraid people would think I was being weak or even pathetic if I cried in public.

I remember when Bill and I visited the farmhouse once when the tenant still lived there. The gentleman living there had lost his wife and was moving into an apartment, and though we planned to move in eventually, Bill had not yet been discharged from the army. The tenant allowed us to look around unaccompanied and even let us go upstairs.

"Go ahead," he waved his hand. "I'll wait down here." He was unshaven, his dingy T-shirt crumpled under wide-banded, red suspenders. He scratched the back of his head and sat down.

This will be our home someday, I thought as we climbed the narrow staircase to the second floor. To my surprise, dresses bunched on the pegs in the hallway, and curlers still cluttered the dresser. My skin crawled at the sight of a worn pink nighty left at the end of a bed now occupied by a grungy cat. Slippers waited on a braided rug littered with neglect. Nothing had been moved since she died ... more than five years before.

"I don't go upstairs anymore—no need to." He looked away and cleared his throat. This gruff old soul was avoiding the entire second story of his house. Was it because the pain was too great to face? Or did he fear that removing her things would erase his memory of her? Would things be different if he had someone in his life to help? Or did he push them all away for fear of appearing vulnerable?

Avoidance too often robs us of living fully in the present and keeps us stuck in grief. Isolating oneself, like this widower did, is not the only sign. Other indications can be throwing oneself into a job or projects, over scheduling to stay busy, or acting as if everything is fine when it's not.

In the beginning, grief can be almost unbearable, but eventually we all have to learn to manage our emotions and move forward. Avoidance won't make the pain go away—it only postpones it. We don't have to face our grief alone. The Lord is our burden-bearer and our comforter. He will help us face every aspect of the things we so wish to ignore.

The good news is, however long it takes, when we face those things we've been avoiding, it rewires our brain for healing. We move forward. As we stop running from the painful parts, we somehow come away feeling clean, and we've taken one more step on our journey to healing.

CHAPTER FORTY-FIVE

Have You done your best?
. . . Then be at peace.

Bamma's Blessing

Bamma came home from rehabilitation at St. John's Home in Rochester, but she wasn't ever the same. Her tragic fall was too much to recover from. Just a few weeks after she returned, she suffered a stroke. I've never seen anything like it. I watched the entire right side of her body simply stop working. We got her to the hospital as quickly as possible, and for the third time she was sent back to St. John's. She couldn't speak or feed herself. After every attempt to rehabilitate her failed, she was scheduled to go to another floor of the hospital for hospice care.

My son Kyle is a very big man. He has worked all levels of construction for years and his hands are massive. To see this huge man bending over the bed of his grandmother, day after day, was an illustration of the love of Jesus like I've never seen before. To see those massive hands wiping her chin, giving her tiny tastes of soup, dwarfing her frail, little body was a picture I will never forget. Sometimes he slept all night in the chair next to her bed. I was there almost every day, but it was clear that Kyle had a God-sized anointing for the care she needed. Kyle needed to leave for a while, so I was sitting with her. She seemed agitated with him gone.

"I'm here, Bamma. Kyle had to go somewhere but he'll be back very soon."

I studied her as she slept. I wasn't sure she could hear me, but I said, "We've been through it, Bamma. Haven't we? We've had our struggles, but we've become good, good friends. You have taught me so much about life. You never wanted me to call you mother, but you were a mother to me. You are a wise woman, and the most generous person I've ever known. I love you, Bamma. You're work is done, you can go home now and be with Jesus, and your son."

She raised her fingers and I knew she was trying to reach for me. I took her hand.

With a strained whisper, she managed to ask me a question.

"Have you done the best you can?"

At first I wasn't sure what she was referring to. Then I understood.

"Yes, Bamma, I have."

She paused. Then with a much stronger voice she uttered the last words I would ever hear her speak. "Then be at peace."

I sat in silence beside her, stunned by her blessing. This was so characteristic of the woman: always, always do your best and, in her own words, "to hell with the hinder parts."

She motioned for water and I left to get a fresh cup. I wasn't away for more than five minutes. When I returned—she was gone.

CHAPTER FORTY-SIX

Shaping Miracles from Broken Pieces

After Bamma passed, it dawned on me that it was the first time since I raised my kids that I was the only person I had to be responsible for.

For months after Bamma died, I'd pour coffee and automatically turn toward her apartment. We had wonderful morning conversations. I missed her deeply, but at the same time, it felt wonderful to be free. I was faithful to my husband's promise to keep her out of a nursing home and so glad I did.

Losing Bamma reignited some grief, because she was the last link to my husband besides our sons. Bamma and I talked about him like no one else could. She remembered stories, names and dates intimate to Bill's history. She also was the last to remember details about the farm when Grandma Stevens lived here.

One morning I walked into her vacant apartment and the Lord spoke to me: "This is your new art studio."

The thought actually startled me, because I'd never imagined I would have anything more than a corner in the garage.

"But Lord, I need to rent this for income."

His immediate reply was, "Trust me."

At first, I just stood there stunned. Then ideas began to trickle into my mind. *I can put my antique cabinet over here, and the shelves can go there, and my art table will fit in front of the picture window.* I could see the whole layout.

Over the next week, I moved my art supplies out of my corner in the garage and settled into my beautiful new studio with high ceilings and even a skylight. We'd planned Bamma's apartment so she could have lots of light, however, she had preferred to keep all the heavy drapes drawn. It was a joy to finally remove all those curtains, wash the windows, and let in every drop of sunshine.

Lord, you'll have to make me a better artist to deserve a place like this.

The studio was so awesome I couldn't imagine it was a blessing for me alone, so I started inviting other artists to come once a week and work together on our creations. I served homemade soup and we'd eat, chat, and work on our projects. The fellowship was rich and stirred our creativity. It also helped me with loneliness. Social activities aren't always easy to find. You can only go out to eat just so much. I could see our art group becoming an organized fellowship for Christian artists. We named it *My Creative Hands Community.* I could see us hosting art events for homeschooled kids or groups of women. The group consensus was that our purpose was to ignite creativity.

My dearest art buddy, Cindy, had a vision for a compilation of inspirational art and prose to be placed in cancer treatment centers. Artists from around the world contributed their artwork and soon the book *A Hug of Compassion* was born.

The same passion I once had for singing was now being expressed through art and writing. Each day, I began my morning by writing and concluded the day doing art. I dug out the primitive, homemade books I'd made for my grandkids and created fresh illustrations. Gradually, they were finished. Finding a publisher for children's picture books is very difficult for a new author, so I decided to start my own publishing company: Mim's Pickety Press.

I kept thinking about other widows and how I might help them through their journey. I decided to invite all the widows in my church to a tea at my house. My studio was transformed into a shabby chic tea room and I even brought out Bamma's teacup collection. Eight widows came.

As I pondered having another tea, some of the obstacles we'd faced with the first tea discouraged my plans, things like parking, bathroom accessibility, and slippery walkways.

I kept thinking about the new community center in our town, but was fairly certain it would cost too much. Then one day the Lord prompted me to inquire.

"We charge $100," said the secretary.

I put my head down and thought for a moment.

"What's this for?" she asked.

Her face lit up when I told her it was for a widow's fellowship. "How about $20 a month?"

I signed a lease that day, not knowing who would come, if they'd come, and what we would do. I only knew that God was inspiring something bigger than I could comprehend, and confirmed it with the price.

"What's the name of your group?"

I had no idea. I hadn't thought that far.

"We'll just put it under your name," she said.

As I prayed, the Lord clarified the purpose of this group. It was not a grief group, but to help women keep moving forward. That's when I knew what the name would be Lives Overcoming Loss (L.O.L.), because in Christ, we can overcome anything.

We had our first meeting in the new building in 2015. My daughter-in-law had suggested I ask each woman to bring a dish to pass.

"Women are givers," she said. "It will be a good ice-breaker, and give them a chance to cook something they probably wouldn't cook just for themselves."

As she predicted, the first women to attend covered two eight-foot tables with every imaginable entree, salad, and dessert. We sang, shared, prayed, and even had a guest speaker. We had 12 ladies, women of all ages, from different churches all over our area.

The joyful sound of chatter echoed through that community room. Everyone was talking, no one was being left out. There were smiles and laughter, even for the few who cried.

When the last widow waved goodbye, I sat alone in the room and thought back to the years of grief. *It's happening, Lord. The broken pieces are being shaped into a miracle to bless others.*

I've made it through the wilderness, Lord. I'm a better woman because of You. I'm wiser, more patient, I have greater endurance, and creativity ... Your faithfulness and gentleness have led me and taught me through every difficulty. All the glory and praise goes to You.

There was one thing unresolved. I was attending a very large church, and though it was dynamic with rich teaching, I didn't feel as if I fit there anymore. One Sunday I decided to visit a small church only five minutes from my house. When I walked into the church, the first two people I saw were widows from my L.O.L. group! Several Sundays later, I learned that a member of the church had passed. Pastor Boldt announced funeral arrangements, then proceeded to talk about grief and what to say or not say to those grieving. In all the years I've been attending church, I have never once heard a pastor prepare his people like he did. As a matter of fact, I'd never heard one sermon on loss or widows, or the journey through grief. I knew this was where I needed to be.

When I talked with the pastor afterwards, he shared that he and his wife had lost their teenage son to cancer.

"I get it," he said.

I could see the miracles from *his* broken pieces, too.

A year later, I learned about the church's annual trip to Ukraine. Pastor Boldt had been going there for more than 25 years. I instantly had the desire to go, but the Lord had to confirm it.

"Do you think I should go—at my age?" I asked a much older widow.

She promptly blew a raspberry, and said, "Too old? You're young yet. If you don't want to go, I'll go for you."

I wanted to be so sure it was the Lord. It sounded exciting, but was it the exciting thing God wanted me to do? Before I made my final decision, I happened to visit a church that hosting a speaker I wanted to hear. When I walked into the lobby, a stranger walked up to me and said, "The Lord has just told me you have an international anointing on your life." The stranger didn't know me or anything about me.

I knew it was my confirmation, so the next day I called my pastor and enlisted to join the mission team.

As the trip approached, I began to have dreams where I was singing in front of groups of Ukrainians. I pushed that thought out of my mind because I hadn't played my guitar or sung in years. But the pictures kept coming.

Hesitantly, I dusted off my guitar and tuned it.

When I started to sing, out came the voice I'd remembered. I sang as if no time had passed, like I'd never had an accident. Best of all, there was no pain!

As I sang alone in my studio, the anointing of the Holy Spirit descended upon me. My throat felt well-oiled and young. Tears of joy trickled down my face. "Lord, please don't let this be my imagination. Don't let me get my hopes up if this isn't what You want. I'm content not to sing."

But instead, the desire to sing returned. At the first meeting in Ukraine, I told my story, picked up my guitar, and out came my voice, clear and painless. It was not the voice of a woman my age. It was if I'd never stopped singing. Each meeting my voice got stronger. At the last gathering, in a little gypsy church, I sang the song I may have been best known for, "Sparrow Song," and was able to finish it with effortless yodeling.

Fibromyalgia was also in remission. The farther away from stress I got, and the closer to Jesus, the less I've been sidelined by aches and pains. Another miracle was the lack of anxiety. I no longer rise in the morning with a rush of angst. I've learned that whenever I have a little anxiety, I pray for those who are sufferers. It has completely turned mine around.

It has been 10 years since Bill died. Everything I've shared about God's faithfulness is true. He is in the process of turning every broken piece into a story to share. I consider my emotional and physical healing a total miracle. This is the gift of God's grace to me, and I choose daily to embrace it.

The farmhouse also has changed. The drafty, old kitchen has been insulated. The cupboards that were once an open highway for mice have been replaced. I bought a wood stove and I get my exercise lugging wood all winter.

Little Molly died a few months after Bamma, but the farmhouse has another fur-ball to love. His name is Oden, a 135-pound German Shepherd. I used to get irritated when Bamma referred to me as Molly's Mommy. Funny, the other day I caught myself saying, "Oden, baby, Mommy's gotta go bye-bye." I'm becoming more and more like Bamma every day. Who could have imagined?

There have been more changes in and around me than I can write. The immeasurable kindness of the Lord has kept me through each moment.

I invite you to find your own place, like my porch swing, to sit and seek comfort from the Lord. As you give the broken pieces of your heart to the Lord, He will wrap each one with His love and give you the miracle of healing and renewed hope.

Gifts for You, from Your Heavenly Father

The following verses are taken from Scripture and personalized as prayers. I use these verses in my quiet time on the porch swing, and they bring deep nourishment to my spirit. May they nourish you, too. I pray you will find your own special quiet place to sit alongside your Helper and be with Him. ~ Marji

Lord, there is nothing compared to the excellence of the knowledge of You (from Philippians 3:8).

Father, I thank You for the Holy Spirit in my life. Thank You that He is doing a work in me, to produce Your fruitfulness which is love, joy, peace, patience, kindness, goodness, faithfulness, gentleness, and self-control (from Galatians 5:22).

I trust in your unfailing love, Lord; my heart rejoices in the salvation You have given me through Christ Jesus (from Psalm 13:5).

Lord, You are the rock I cling to. You are my fortress and my deliverer. I take refuge in You, my God. You are my shield and my stronghold (from Psalm 18:2).

Lord, thank You for the glory and excellence You have given to us through Your Son, Jesus. Thank you for Your precious, magnificent promises, so that by them we can become partakers of Your divine nature (from 2 Peter 4).

Father, thank You that You are making me a virtuous woman, one who shows the active quality of excellence. I ask that the work of my hands will always bring You praise and glory (from Proverbs 31:31).

Lord, help me to trust in You and do good; to dwell in the land, the circle of influence where You have placed me, and to cultivate faithfulness there. Show me how to delight myself in You, Lord; and assure me that when I delight in You, You will give me the desires of my heart, ones that reflect the desires of Yours.

Help me commit my way to You, Lord, to trust also in You, and believe that You will do it. Help me be confident that You will bring forth righteousness as the light and judgment as the noonday. Lord, show me how to rest in You, and wait patiently for You (from Psalm 37:4-7).

Help me to always trust in You, Lord, for You are my everlasting Rock (from Isaiah 16:4).

Lord, You are my strength in time of trouble (from Psalm 37:39).

You give power to the weak, and when I have no might, You will increase my strength (from Isaiah 40:29).

You, Lord, are a shield around me. You are my glory, and the One who lifts my head (from Psalm 3:3.)

You make my heart glad and you fill me with rejoicing, my body also will rest secure (from Psalm 16:9).

You will put a new song in my mouth, a hymn of praise to You. I will praise Your name in song and glorify You with thanksgiving (from Psalm 40:3, and Psalm 69:30).

Thank you, Lord, that when I lack wisdom, I can ask You, and you will give it generously to me (from James 1:5).

Thank you, Lord, that when I submit my ways to You, You will make my path straight (from Proverbs 3:6).

Help me to remember Your marvelous works which You have done in my life. Help me never forget Your wonders and the words of Your mouth (from 1 Chronicles 16:12).

You remembered me in my weakness, Father. Your faithful love endures forever (from Psalm 136:23).

When I remember Your word, Lord, I am comforted (from Psalm 119:52).

Help me, Lord, to think on things that are true and honest, things that are just, things that are pure and lovely. Help me to set my mind on things that are of good report, things that are virtuous and praiseworthy (from Philippians 4:8).

You have promised to keep me in perfect peace, when my mind is set on You (from Isaiah 26:3).

You are ... my shield (Genesis 15:1-3).

You are ... God Almighty (Genesis 17:1, 35:11).

You are ... compassionate (Exodus 22:27).

You are ... holy (Leviticus 11:44).

You are ... my portion and my inheritance (Numbers 18:20).

You are... my salvation (Psalm 35:3).

You are ... with me (Isaiah 41:10, 43:5, Jeremiah 1:19,15:20, Matthew 28:20).

You are ... the Lord, besides You there is no salvation (Isaiah 43:11).

You are ... the first and the last (Isaiah 44:6, Revelation 1:17).

You are ... He who comforts (Isaiah 5:12).

You are ... merciful (Jeremiah 3:12).

You are ... a father (Jeremiah 31:9).

You are ... my inheritance (Ezekiel 44:28).

You are ... gentle and lowly of heart (Matthew 11:29).

You are ... the God of Abraham, Isaac, and Jacob (Matthew 22:32).

You are ... the Christ (Mark 14:61-63).

You are ... the Bread of Life (John 6:48).

You are ... the Light of the world (John 8:12).

You are ... not of this world (John 8:24).

You are ... the Good Shepherd (John 10:1).

You are ... the door (John 10:9).

You are ... the son of God (John 10:36).

You are ... the resurrection and the life (John 11:25).

You are ... teacher and Lord (John 13:13).

You are ... the Way, the Truth, and the Life (John 14:1).

You are ... the true vine (John 15:1).

You are ... the Alpha and Omega (Revelation 1:8).

You are ... alive forevermore (Revelation 1:18).

You are ... coming soon (Revelation 3:11).

You are ... the bright morning star (Revelation 22:16).

You are ... the LORD, my God (quoted throughout Scripture).

I trust You, Father. My confidence is in You. Make me like a tree planted by the water that sends out its roots toward the stream. Remind me I should not fear when heat comes, for my leaves will always be green. Assure me I should have no worries in a year of drought, because I will never fail to bear fruit (from Jeremiah 17:7-8).

Oh Lord, help me to grow in trust with all my heart and not lean on my own understanding. Help me to acknowledge You in all my ways, believing that You will make my paths straight (from Proverbs 3:5-6).

Father, let each morning bring me word of Your unfailing love. Show me the way that I should go, for I entrust You with my life. Thank you, Lord (from Psalm 143:8).

Lord, remind me that when I dwell in the shelter of the Most High, I will rest in the shadow of the Almighty. Help me know that You are my refuge and my fortress, Lord (from Psalm 91:1-2).

Father, I am confident that You will meet all my needs according to the riches of Your glory in Christ Jesus (from Philippians 4:19).

You are with me, Lord, therefore, I have no need to fear or be dismayed. You are my God, and I know You will strengthen me and help me. I am confident You will even hold me by Your righteous right hand. Thank you, Father. (from Isaiah 41:10).

You, Lord, are a shield around me. You are the One who lifts my head (from Psalm 3:3).

Teach me, Lord, to always do Your will, for You are my God; may Your Holy Spirit lead me on level ground, secure in Your arms. Thank you for this hope (from Psalm 143:10).

Father, I believe that You will make known to me every path I am to take. Grant me the joy of Your presence and the pleasure of living with You (from Psalm 16:11).

Thank You, Father, that You work things for my good and that Your grace causes me to abound with thanksgiving that brings You glory. Help me understand I should not lose heart ... for this trial is producing an eternal weight of glory far beyond all comparison (from 2 Corinthians 4:14-17).

Lord, thank You that even though I am shaken, Your kingdom cannot be shaken. Help me to please You by offering You my grateful worship in reverence and awe (from Hebrews 12:28).

Since the creation of the world, Lord, Your invisible attributes, eternal power, and divine nature have been clearly seen. Help me never become one who knows You, but does not honor You as God, or give thanks (from Romans 1:20-21).

Lord, You strengthen and protect me. Help me to trust You with all my heart. You have rescued me, and my heart is full of joy; I will sing to You, Oh my God, with a song of gratitude (from Psalm 28:7).

Father, help me to give thanks in all circumstances, for this is Your will for me, since I am in Christ Jesus (from 1 Thessalonians 5:18).

Father, help me to always be grateful and give thanks, for You are good, and Your love endures forever (from 1 Chronicles 16:34).

Lord, show me how to enter Your gates with thanksgiving and Your courts with praise (from Psalm 100:4).

Lord, You say in Your Word that a broken spirit dries up the bones and a joyful heart is good medicine. Please give me Your joy, I pray (from Proverbs 17:22).

Lord, Your Word says a joyful heart makes my countenance cheerful, but a sad heart reflects a broken spirit. Heal me, O Lord. Give me a joyful heart once again (from Proverbs 15:13).

Father, You filled the mouths of your people with laughter, and their tongues with songs of joy. Please do the same for me, so that just as it was said among the nations, "The LORD has done great things for them," others can say this of me, too (from Psalm 126:2).

Lord, remind me that You will fill my mouth with laughter and my lips with shouts of joy (from Job 8:21).

Father, Your Word says that there is a time for everything, and a season for every activity under the heavens: a time to be born and a time to die, a time to plant and a time to uproot, a time to kill and a time to heal, a time to tear down and a time to build, a time to weep and a time to laugh, a time to mourn and a time to dance ... Help me to trust Your timing, and to learn to be content in the season You have me in right now (from Ecclesiastes 3:1-4, NIV).

Lord, my soul is hungry—please feed me until I am satisfied. Lord, I am mourning—please comfort me and help me to laugh again ... in Your time, I pray (from Luke 6:21).

You are the true vine, Lord, and Your Father is the vineyard keeper. You prune and tend me so that I will produce much fruit ... Help me to abide in You, because I cannot bear fruit by myself ... Help me to keep Your commandments, and abide in Your love just as You did, Lord, with Your Father. Let me partake of Your joy and bring You glory, I pray. (from John 15:1-11)

Father, remind me that the joy of the Lord is my strength (from Nehemiah 8:10b).

Help me to seek first Your Kingdom, and Your righteousness, Lord. Help me not to worry about what to eat, or drink, or wear, and remind me that when I place you first in my life, You will provide everything I need (from Matthew 6:31-33).

Father, help me learn how to be still and know that You are God ... (from Psalm 46:10).

Father, thank You that when I draw near to You, You will draw near to me (from James 4:8).

Father, Your Word says that Jesus rebuked the winds and the waves, and it became completely calm. Please rebuke the winds and quiet the storms in my life (from Matthew 8:26).

Lord, I can cry out to You in my trouble, and You will bring me out of my distress. You will still the storm to a whisper; and hush the waves of the sea. I give thanks to You, Lord, for Your unfailing love and Your wonderful deeds for me (from Psalm 107:28-31).

Father, my soul finds rest in You alone, for You are my salvation ... Hide me under the shadow of Your wing, for in You alone do I put my trust, (from Psalm 91:1-4).

Lord, help me not to be anxious about anything, but in everything, to learn to pray with great thanksgiving because You hear me and answer me. Remind me that Your peace completely transcends my understanding. Assure me that Your peace will guard my heart and mind in Christ Jesus (from Philippians 4:6-7).

When I face trials of any kind, Lord, remind me that the testing of my faith produces perseverance. Help me to understand that You desire perseverance to finish its work in me so that I may be mature and complete, not lacking anything. When I need wisdom, Lord, I believe that You will give it to me generously (from James 1:1-2).

A Word of Thanks

"And in this I rejoice. Yes, and I will continue to rejoice, because I know that through your prayers and the provision of the Spirit of Jesus Christ, my distress will turn out for my deliverance" (Philippians 1:19, NIV)

It's difficult to list all the hands that play a part in the making of a book. It's like the kaleidoscope of an October maple tree bursting with color—no one leaf stands alone. It's a symphony of tone—one flutter of encouragement at a time.

Perhaps it started back when I discovered that writing was a way to entertain myself beside fly fishing streams in the Colorado wilderness while Bill fished. Perhaps it took hold the day I poured out my grief to a dear saint, Sharon Evans, and she looked into my tear-streaked face and said, "Write that book." Perhaps it grew through my cherished friendship with Cindy, or Jeanine, Janet or Jerry, Rachel or Susan who've listened to my dream to write and encouraged me to hone my craft and keep going.

Certainly, it was my Christian writer's critique group, Word Weavers, who taught me so much about the mechanics of writing, along with the patient professionalism of my editor and friend, Rachel Dewey. I know it includes the prayers of many in secret.

Thank you to my sons Kyle and Jonathan who have always been a touch of Jesus with skin on. Thank you to my daughter-in-law, Autumn, for being an important sounding board, especially during the first two years of widowhood. Thank you to Bernice, for the hundreds of hours of good conversation and wisdom. Thank you to my seven grandchildren who have blessed me with hours of laughter and inspiration, and who have buoyed my heart with their endless energy and joy. Thank you to my faithful neighbor, Coleen, who hung with the Stevens family through so much. Thank you to the women of Lives Overcoming Loss (L.O.L.) who have allowed me to pour into their lives, and have stood with me as this ministry has developed.

From seed to fruition my desire has always been clear—to be an encouragement to those who know what it's like to endure loss, to hold up the broken pieces of their hearts to a God often veiled in the mystery of suffering and dare to hope for healing. It is the loving hand of Jesus who puts the passion in our heart to do good, and the courage to step out for a task much greater than ourselves.

~ Marji

About the Author

Marji Stevens is a joyful exhorter, creative storyteller and engaging Bible teacher. After 30 years of ministry as a singer-songwriter, Marji lost her ability to sing following an accident that resulted in fibromyalgia. Returning to her roots as an artist, Marji found her creativity branching out in new ways. After losing Bill, her husband of 40 years, in 2007, Marji continued drawing, painting, and writing. She has since written, illustrated, and published six children's books and collaborated with artist-friend Cindy Dalton on *Hug of Compassion*, an art book for those going through cancer. Her first nonfiction book, *Gifts from the Porch Swing*, has been a labor of love for widows and others facing loss. Marji leads Embracing Grace Ministries and is the founder of Lives Overcoming Loss (L.O.L.). She shares her art, humor, books, and more at **marjistevens.com,** where she also offers Biblical truth and inspiration through her blog. A mother to two grown sons and grandmother of seven, Marji resides in a 200-year-old farmhouse in the rolling hills of western New York.

Mim's Pickety Press

From Mim's Pickety Press comes humorous, gentle, and inspirational children's books written and illustrated by Marji Stevens, known as "Mimmy" to her grandchildren.

The Little Clock that Couldn't Tock

Sometimes our very best efforts are not enough. Tick learns the secret of successful tocking when Ol' Doc Clock arrives with a special gift in answer to her prayers.

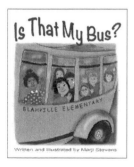

Is That My Bus?

Hazel's first ride on the school bus comes with some wacky surprises. But Hazel learns that good friends and a little encouragement can make courage grow.

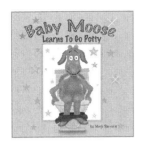

Baby Moose
Learns to Go Potty

Baby Moose learns a big lesson and wins
a prize for not being afraid to try.

Baby Moose and the
Shiny Red Fireman Hat

Baby Moose learns that one mishap doesn't
have to ruin the whole day. Sometimes, a day
of doubt may end with a wonderful surprise.

Baby Moose
in Blahville

Baby Moose learns that God answers
prayer—sometimes in the most
unusual ways.

Find these books and more at:
MarjiStevens.com

Lives
Overcoming Loss

In response to the Lord's call in James 1:27 to care for widows, Embracing Grace Ministries formed a monthly fellowship called Lives Overcoming Loss (L.O.L.). Since its launch in 2015, L.O.L. has expanded to include ministry to divorced women as well. For more information on this ministry or to work with Marji to form a local chapter of L.O.L, please visit: LivesOvercomingLoss.org

Lives Overcoming Loss

You Are Not Alone... *by Marji Stevens*

For times when just a brief page or two is all the newly bereft can process, *Lives Overcoming Loss* may become a welcome balm to the soul. This pocket-sized gift booklet is filled with Scripture verses, inspirational quotes, understanding, and encouragement for the hearts of all those facing loss. Highlighted with full-color art from Marji Stevens' original watercolors and ink drawings, *Lives Overcoming Loss* offers a gentle touch of comfort and hope from the shared perspective of others who have endured the storms of grief.

Available in two versions—one specifically for widows, and another for all mourning the loss of a loved one—this beautiful booklet can be a perfect companion to *Gifts from the Porch Swing* or it can stand alone as a simple blessing for a broken heart.

The mission of Embracing Grace Ministries is to:

- ignite simplicity and devotion in following Jesus Christ.
- encourage the hearts of women in all seasons of life
- inspire and ignite creativity

Embracing Grace Ministries includes:

Lives Overcoming Loss (L.O.L.), a ministry for widows,

Mim's Pickety Press, publishing art and books,

My Creative Hands Community, a fellowship for Christian artists, and

Marji's writing, teaching, and speaking ministry.

Marji is available to lead special events such as creative art workshops, provide Bible teaching, stories, humor and songs at conferences or retreats, or guide support group gatherings for widows and divorcees.

For more information, visit:

EmbracingGraceMinistries.org

marjistevens.com

info@marjistevens.com

Made in the USA
Middletown, DE
06 September 2018